Anger and Stress Management God's Way

Anger and Stress Management God's Way

A Biblical Perspective
on How to Overcome Anger and Stress
Before They Destroy You and Others

Dr. Wayne Mack

Calvary Press Publishing • Greenville, SC
www.calvarypress.com
1-855-2-CALVARY/ (855-222-5827)

Calvary Press Publishing
209 North Main Street #225
Greenville, SC 29601

ISBN-13: 978-1-879737-56-3

    1. Christian Life 2. Christian Counseling 3. Anger Management
    4. Christian Family 5. Applied Theology

Cover and Book Design: Anthony Rotolo

Manufactured in the USA
    3 4 5 6 7 8 9 10   07 08

CONTENTS

Anger and stress are a familiar part of contemporary living. On the news we hear about road rage. We know people who have been subjected to physical abuse. Each year industry invests thousands of dollars in stress management programs to help managers deal with the pressures of life and work. Christians are not immune to these struggles. We have two needs: First, to have applicable passages on anger and stress management identified in the Scriptures. Second, to have them explained to our hungry hearts.

The wise Apostle exhorted his son in the faith, "Do your best to present yourself to God as one approved by him, a worker who has no need to be ashamed, rightly explaining the word of truth"(2 Tim 2:15). This book represents the faithful labors of a pastor, a teacher, and a counselor who has made the mastery of the Scripture the pursuit of his life. Each page of this book references, unfolds, and applies the truth of the Word of God. You can give yourself confidently to the insights and truth you will find here, knowing it reflects the biblical understanding of a safe spiritual guide. If you gain nothing else from reading *Anger and Stress Management God's Way,* you will be exposed to scores of texts that address the problems of anger and stress.

You will gain far more. Not only does Dr. Wayne Mack understand the Bible's teaching about anger, he brings decades of counseling experience to this book. He has obviously listened to and helped people who have been crippled by anger. His insights are not theoretical; they reflect the practical understanding of someone who knows people, the Word of God and the practical art of spiritual warfare.

Some Christian books are heavy on the side of practical tips and light on foundational biblical teaching. This book is different; it provides the reader with both. This is a practical book. It offers responses to anger and stress that are imminently doable and embedded in biblical truth. You will learn how to discern between sinful and holy anger. Dr. Mack supplies the reader with vivid biblical descriptions of the characteristics of sinful anger. He will walk you through responding constructively to anger and train you to know the grace of God to turn from sinful anger. You will learn penetrating questions to help you evaluate and understand your anger. These questions will illuminate the heart issues that push and pull angry responses in life.

You will be amazed at how much the Bible says about stress and its effects on you and others. In two wonderful chapters, Wayne Mack will show you ten factors that will enable you to respond to stress in constructive ways.

The book you are holding looks at anger and stress with straightforward, unvarnished honesty, but retains a hopeful and optimistic confidence in grace. God's people have hope because God has not only given us truth but also enablement. God has revealed truth in the Bible and has empowered his people through the grace of the gospel. There is good news here; God gives us biblical ways to manage anger and stress.

Dr. Ted Tripp,
President of Shepherding Ministries; Author of
Shepherding a Child's Heart; Conference Speaker, and
Pastor of Grace Fellowship Church in Hazeleton, PA

Anger! Stress! These are two words that are used frequently in the course of our daily lives. They're so commonly used because they describe a very common phenomenon. Who of us has not been on the giving and receiving end of anger? Unfortunately, the same is true of stress. We all know people or perhaps we're the people who have been "stressed out." Well, whether it's anger or stress, we are all too familiar with the experience. Who of us has never observed or even been a participant in the devastating consequences of either of these two destroyers?

Yes, I call them destroyers because that's what they are and do. Nothing good has ever come out of mishandled stress or sinful anger. Scripture says, "Wrath is fierce and anger a flood" (Proverbs 27:4). How picturesque and how true is this description of sinful anger. An unbiblical kind of anger is like a flood that destroys people and property. Truly, "the wrath of man does not achieve the righteousness of God" (James 1:20). In fact, it does the opposite. It never does anything good, but it surely does a lot of damage. So we must learn how to control it, or it will destroy us and other people either literally or figuratively.

Likewise, it can be said that stress is much like anger in its effects on the individual and his relationships with people. *Eustress* (good stress—a certain amount of concern) is good, but eustress can quickly and easily become *distress*, which by definition is that which causes sorrow, misery, pain or suffering. The dictionary indicates that stress is closely associated with agony and anguish, with that which causes torment and can be excruciating.

Because of the prevalence of these two problems and the damage they can cause, we are constantly hearing about anger and stress management seminars. Because business executives know of the way that either of these two destroyers can hurt their companies, they regularly contract with so called experts in these areas to come and present seminars to their employees. Legal authorities will sometimes require people who have become threats to other people to go to seminars or take courses on these subjects.

Most of these courses and seminars are based on humanistic approaches to these issues. They completely ignore turning to Scripture for the counsel of our great, all-wise God who is the world's greatest expert on how to handle anger and stress. That this is what the world does in its approach to these issues shouldn't surprise us, but the appalling thing is that many Christians are not aware of the fact that the Bible contains the most valuable, authoritative and trustworthy information about how to handle ungodly anger and stress.

After many years of counseling and study on these subjects, I have written this book to provide the kind of help that is not based on man's opinions, but on the solid truth of God's infallible, relevant Word. I encourage you to read it carefully, look up and study the Scriptures used and answer the study questions that are included for every chapter. Then, evaluate your own life and behavior using the material in this book as an evaluative grid. Finally, confess your sins and ask God and others you have sinned against for their forgiveness, seek the help of God for change where you need to change, and put the principles of this book into practice in your life. You don't have to be overcome and destroyed by ungodly anger or stress. By God's grace, you can be an overcomer.

SOMETIMES IT'S RIGHT AND SOMETIMES IT'S WRONG TO BE ANGRY

Is it always a sin to be angry? Some people sincerely believe that it's always a sin to be angry. From childhood, they were taught that it was wrong to express anger in any form. Yet there are others that seem to believe that anger is never sinful—unless it's directed at them.

For example, some parents will not tolerate their children expressing anger at them or each other, but will quickly excuse their own anger towards their children. There are husbands and wives who have one standard for themselves and another standard for their spouses. A man once told me that his anger against his wife was always justified. These people think that anger is wrong mostly when it's someone else's anger, but not their own.

The truth of the matter is that *anger is sometimes sinful and sometimes righteous*. Ephesians 4:31 says, "Let all bitterness and wrath and anger and clamor and slander be put away from you, along with all malice." In other words, let every kind—all forms—of anger and wrath be put away. Colossians 3:8 teaches the same. "But now you also, put them all aside: anger, wrath, malice, slander and abusive speech from your mouth."

According to these verses, there is a kind of anger that is sinful and that must be excluded from the life of a believer. This is the kind of anger we find in Genesis 4 when Cain became angry with his brother Abel and murdered him. In I Samuel 18, Saul was angry with David when David did well in battle and was praised by the people. Later, Saul became angry with his son Jonathan for being friends with David (I Samuel 20:30). These were all expressions of sinful anger.

In Mark 6:19, we are told that Herodias "had it in" (this is the literal translation from the Greek) for John the Baptist. Because of her sinful anger, John the Baptist was beheaded. In Acts 7:54, it says that the Jewish leaders were enraged against Stephen. As a result of their sinful anger, they took up stones and killed him. In Acts 23:3, the apostle Paul went before the high priest of the Sanhedrin and said, "God is going to strike you, you white-washed wall! Do you sit to try me according to the Law, and in violation of the Law order me to be struck?" The context and Paul's later confession indicate that this was sinful anger on Paul's part. As the Bible indicates in these and many other verses, there are times when our anger is sinful.

The Bible also teaches that there are times when our anger is not sinful. There are times when it's proper, righteous, and necessary to be angry. In the same passage in Ephesians 4 where we are instructed to put aside bitterness, wrath, and anger, we are told that there is a way to be properly angry. Ephesians 4:26 commands, "Be angry, and yet do not sin." It's clear from this verse that there is a kind of anger that is not sinful. These verses do not contradict each other; they simply are teaching us how to handle two different kinds of anger—anger that is sinful and anger that is not sinful.

There are many places in Scripture where it's written that God—who cannot sin—was angry. In Psalm 7:11, it says, "God...has indignation every day." Exodus 4:14 tells us that the anger of God burned against Moses. Deuteronomy 29:27-28 declares, "Therefore, the anger of the Lord burned against that land, to bring upon it every curse which is written in this book; and the Lord uprooted them from their land in anger and in fury and in great wrath, and cast them into another land, as it is this day." God was extremely angry at the Israelites on this and other occasions.

The gospels of Mark and John describe two situations in which the

Lord Jesus, the meek and lowly One, became righteously angry. Mark 3:5 says that He was deeply grieved and became angry because of the Pharisees' hard hearts. We know that Christ's anger was sinless—holy and righteous—because "in Him there is no sin" (I John 3:5). In John 2:13-17, Jesus angrily drove out the sellers and moneychangers from the temple courts because zeal for His Father's house had consumed Him.

Acts 17:16 relates an example of righteous anger on the part of the apostle Paul. While ministering in Philippi, Paul had been beaten, falsely accused, and thrown in prison. His life had been in danger from an earthquake and he had eventually been thrown out of town (Acts 16:16-40). From Philippi, Paul went on to minister in two other cities and was threatened and chased out of both (Acts 17:1-15). Paul arrived in Athens alone and had to wait there for his companions, Timothy and Silas, to join him.

We can only assume that Paul arrived in Athens physically and emotionally exhausted. Very likely, he anticipated a time of rest and recovery while waiting for Timothy and Silas. Though this may have been his intention, the Scripture says that, *his spirit was being provoked within him* as he was observing the city full of idols"(Acts 17:16). *The Expository Dictionary of New Testament Words* indicates that this phrase means that Paul's spirit was roused to anger (Vine, 228). *The Christian Counselor's New Testament* translates the sentence this way: *"His spirit was enraged within him,* as he was beholding the city full of idols." In other words, Paul was righteously angry.

Another example of righteous anger is found in II Corinthians 7:9-11. In his previous letter to the Corinthians, Paul had rebuked the people for various sins. In this passage of his second letter to them, Paul described their response to his first message:

> I now rejoice, not that you were made sorrowful, but that you were made sorrowful to the point of repentance; …For the sorrow that is according to the will of God produces a repentance without regret, leading to salvation…For behold what earnestness this very thing, this godly sorrow, has produced in you: *what vindication of yourselves, what indignation, what fear, what longing, what zeal, what avenging of wrong!*

The believers in Corinth had responded to Paul's teaching both in action and in mind. They took steps to avenge their wrongs and they also became sorrowful over their sin to the point of zealous indignation, or anger. Paul commended them for their anger because it was for the right reason and because it was expressed rightly. In essence, he said to them, "Good job! I'm glad you became angry over your sin."

The passages that we have just looked at clearly indicate that there are two kinds of anger. There is a sinful kind of anger that is destructive and ungodly and there is a righteous kind of anger that is constructive and godly. What, then, distinguishes godly anger from ungodly anger? When is our anger sinful and when is it righteous? How can we be sure that our anger is used constructively rather than destructively?

To answer these questions, we need to first carefully study the characteristics of sinful anger—anger that is displeasing to God and destructive to us, other people, and other things. We will study these characteristics in the rest of this chapter and all of chapter two. In chapters three and four, we will consider how to respond to our anger in a way that is godly and constructive.

APPLICATION QUESTIONS

» What do you think about the idea that anger is sometimes righteous and sometimes sinful?
» What biblical statements support the concept of righteous anger?
» Which of the two types of anger do you think occurs more frequently?
» Which of the two types of anger do you think you experience more frequently?
» What biblical examples of righteous anger were given in the previous section?

WHEN IS OUR ANGER SINFUL?
WHAT ARE THE CHARACTERISTICS OF SINFUL ANGER?

Our anger is sinful when we become angry for the wrong reasons. In many cases, our anger is aroused because of our *selfishness.* Selfish anger is always a sin. Cain's anger toward his brother Abel was a sinfully selfish anger (Genesis 4). Cain had not brought a proper sacrifice to the Lord and when God rejected his offering, Cain became angry with God and jealous of his brother. His anger was caused by his offering being rejected by God—selfishness—and his brother's offering being accepted—jealousy. When we become angry because someone else is receiving attention or appreciation that we are not, our anger is sinful. If we are honest, we will recognize how frequently we get angry for this reason!

In I Kings 21, Ahab became sinfully angry because of his selfishness. Ahab, the king of Israel, wanted to buy the vineyard of a man named Naboth. Naboth refused to sell it, angering King Ahab. The Bible says, "So Ahab came into his house sullen and vexed..." (21:4). In other words, he was depressed (sullen) and angry (vexed). In my experience with counseling, I have found that depression and anger often go together as one frequently leads to the other. Ahab was angry because he was denied the vineyard that his heart coveted and that he thought he had a right to. How often do we become angry because our "rights" have been denied?

Some time ago, I got on an elevator and made an effort to be friendly to another person riding with me. I gave the man standing beside me a cheerful "Hello" and asked him, "How are you doing today?" The man ignored me; he never blinked an eye or acknowledged my greeting. He never answered my question. He just flat out ignored me. My reaction to his lack of response was a bit of irritation. I thought, "Who does he think he is, treating me like that?" I interpreted his non-response as a put down and a slap in the face. In my sinful pride, I started to become angry.

At the time I wouldn't have called it that. If I admitted that I was at all affected by that little episode I would have probably used some euphemisms such as, "I was hurt or a little upset or mildly disturbed at being snubbed that way." After all, I was nice to him. I went out of my way to show an interest in him. I thought that I deserved a certain amount of politeness. I never considered that he might have had a lot on his mind; a problem with his hearing, a severe headache, or that he was reticent to interact with strangers. I just assumed that I had a "right" to be acknowledged, and that he was denying that right. When I was denied that perceived right, I experienced a mild form of anger. I thought I had a right for him to recognize me. I thought I had a right for him to treat me as though I was worthwhile, as though I was important enough that he should at least respond to me. That's what happened with Ahab, and that's what frequently happens with us. Though my expression and experience was not as severe as that of Ahab's in I Kings 21, it was still the same species and it had its roots in the same soil of pride and selfishness. That kind of response is sinful, selfish anger.

When children fail to do something exactly as their parents want them to do it, even if their actions are not definitively sinful, parents sometimes become angry. After all, they think, "Children are supposed to obey and show respect to their parents. And the fact that they didn't do something exactly as I wanted them to do shows disrespect." Never mind that the Bible says, "love suffers long and is kind…love is not provoked" (I Corinthians 13:4-5). Their children have not treated them the way they want to be treated. So they become peeved and upset and openly express their annoyance to their children. When that happens, the parent's anger has nothing to do with what is best for the children. It's simply due to the fact that they're not doing what they want them to do. They become upset because, as the boss of their home, their "rights" are being denied. That kind of anger is sinful, selfish anger.

The anger of Herodias against John the Baptist was a sinful, selfish anger. She was upset with John the Baptist because he had told her that she was sinning by living with her husband's brother. Herodias did not want to hear the truth about her sinful lifestyle because she felt that she had a "right" to live as she pleased. Likewise, Saul's anger against David was sinfully selfish. When Saul heard the women singing, "Saul has slain his thousands, and David his ten thousands" (I Samuel 18:7), the Bible says that Saul, from that time forward, was angry with David. He was jealous of the praise and recognition that David was getting. His anger was sinfully selfish.

How frequently do we become angry when someone else receives more credit than we do? We may think about how regularly we attend church services, how dedicated we are to serving others, how faithfully we teach Sunday School classes week after week, or how much money we give to the work of the church. Then, when someone else is recognized in some way in the church more than we are, we respond with sinful, selfish anger. "It's not fair! I deserve recognition too!"

In Luke 15:11-32, Jesus told the parable of the prodigal son. In this parable, a young man treated his father unfairly. He demanded his inheritance and then ran away from home with it. He wasted the money on wicked living, quickly using it up. After hitting rock bottom and realizing that he had nowhere else to turn, he returned home. His father welcomed him back with open arms, dressed him in fine clothes, and threw a big party to celebrate his son's return. But when his older brother found out what his father had done, he became resentful and angry. He refused to even come into the house. Why? He was hurt by his father's attention to his younger brother and jealous of the honor that he was receiving. In other words, he was selfishly angry.

Our anger is always sinful when it's caused by our selfishness. Whether we have had our feelings hurt, or we are jealous, or we are not getting recognition, or we believe that our "rights" are being denied, all these things lead to sinful, selfish anger.[1] In the application exercise that follows this paragraph, I will include a practical application study from my book, *A Homework Manual for Biblical Living, Volume 1* that will help to identify how this issue of denied "rights" might be part of an anger problem.

APPLICATION QUESTIONS

» What did the statement mean that our anger is sinful when we become angry for the wrong reason?
» Identify the reason for being angry that makes our anger sinful.
» What does the issue of rights have to do with sinful anger?
» Which of the following do you consider to be your "rights"?
- Right to have and control personal belongings
- Right to privacy
- Right to have and express personal opinions
- Right to earn and use money
- Right to plan your own schedule
- Right to respect from others and to be obeyed by others
- Right to have and choose friends
- Right to belong, be loved, be accepted
- Right to be understood and to be treated fairly
- Right to make own decisions and determine your own future
- Right to be successful
- Right to have good health
- Right to date/be married
- Right to have children
- Right to be considered worthwhile and important
- Right to security and safety
- Right to travel

- Right to have the job you want
- Right to a good education
- Right to be a beautiful person and to be desired
- Right to have fun and to be free of problems
- Right to raise your children your way

» Which of these "rights" are you being denied, and by whom? Discern which "rights" you think are being denied or neglected when you start to become angry. Do you think you have a right to be "respected" and is that why you are becoming annoyed at someone when that person doesn't show you respect? Do you think you have a right to be "appreciated" and is that why you are becoming resentful toward someone who has criticized you or not shown appreciation toward you? Think through the list of "rights" listed previously and identify the ones that that are most important to you; also reflect on how you tend to respond when these so called "rights" are withheld from you.

» Add any other items to this "rights" list that are important and can be problematic to you.

» Consciously recognize that, if you are a Christian, you and all you have and are (your rights included) belong to God (I Cor. 6:19; Rom. 12:1; Ps. 24:1). You are not your own. You belong to Him. He knows what you really need (Philippians 4:19). Trust Him to take care of you and provide for you whatever you need. Believe that God is much wiser than you. Acknowledge this and dedicate all that you are and have, including your "rights" to God. Trust Him to take care of His property. Cease to think in terms of your "rights" and concentrate on God's will and purpose and promises. Make it a point to specifically dedicate your "rights" to God on a regular basis.

» Turning your so-called "rights" over to God doesn't mean you must become a doormat. It doesn't mean that you never make your desires known, or that you never oppose, rebuke, insist, exhort or seek to correct a person. It does mean that you seek to do what you do in a biblical, God-honoring fashion and that you do it for biblical, unselfish reasons, out of biblical, God-honoring motives. It does mean that after you have done all that you may legitimately do, you leave the results with God and believe that He will bring to pass what is right and good for you. It means you believe God's promise that those who fear the Lord shall not lack any good thing (Psalm 34:8-10). It means that you must fulfill your biblical responsibilities and then be content to leave your "rights" to God. It means that you will choose to think of what you formerly considered as "rights" as privileges.

Our anger is sinful when we allow our anger to control us. Proverbs 16:32 says, "He who is slow to anger is better than the mighty, and *he who rules his spirit, than he who captures a city.*" In other words, a person who controls his anger is better than a conquering general. Indeed, it's often harder to conquer our own passions than to conquer a city. Proverbs 25:28 declares, "Like a city that is broken into and without walls is a man who has no control over his spirit." An uncontrolled spirit can be as destructive to our souls as an attacking army is to a city.

These verses are warning us against being people who are controlled by their spirit, which is partly the emotions, rather than being in control of their spirit. Indeed, we usually find it easier to allow the emotion of anger to control us, rather than maintaining control of our anger. How often have we heard someone say (or said it ourselves), "I was so angry, I just couldn't help myself!"? What is this person saying? In reality, they're excusing themselves for being out of control, and from the actions that resulted from their anger. They're claiming no responsibility for what they did because they were at the mercy of their anger. The truth, of course, is that their actions were sinful. Anytime that we allow our anger to control us, we are sinning.

This is precisely what happened to King Ahab. When Ahab did not get what he wanted, he became angry. Instead of accepting Naboth's refusal and going about his duties as ruler of the country, he went to his bedroom and stewed in his anger. Later, Ahab's anger led to the death of Naboth by the conniving of Jezebel, Ahab's wife. Ahab was controlled by his anger rather than in control of his anger.

By way of application, let's consider this scenario. A certain man likes things to be neat and orderly. He likes his house to be cleaned up when he's there. He has expressed his wishes to his wife: a neat house, a neat yard. He has asked that the children's toys be put away and the family room not be left in shambles at the end of the day. He has asked that the children's bicycles not be left all over the front yard, the back yard, and especially the driveway.

One night, this man comes home after a difficult day at work. As he approaches his house, he notices that the yard is full of toys. As he attempts to pull in the driveway, he finds that it's blocked by several bicycles. Seeing that his express wishes for the yard and driveway have not been followed, he starts to become sinfully angry. As he moves the bikes and pulls into the driveway, he recites to himself what he has asked of his wife countless times: "Keep the yard and the driveway cleaned up." By the time he enters the house, he is stewing in his anger. Determined not to say anything to his wife, he greets her with a peck on the cheek, grunts a "hello," and heads down to the family room to cool off.

The family room, of course, is also a mess. Toys are everywhere and he cannot even sit down. His anger is now full-blown, and as he clears off his favorite chair, he thinks to himself, "She doesn't pay any attention to what I say. She knows that I think this is important. She doesn't respect me as the head of this home. I'm under tremendous pressure at work and when I come home, all I want is some peace and quiet and a semblance of order. I can't handle this mess. Why doesn't she think about what I want?" For the rest of the night, he stews and sulks silently, ignoring his family.

What happened here? This man was controlled by his anger. He allowed his spirit to rule his actions, rather than ruling his spirit as he ought to have done. Whenever we allow our anger to dictate how we act to keep us from fulfilling our biblical responsibilities, our anger is sinful.

APPLICATION QUESTIONS

» What did the statement mean that our anger is sinful when we allow it to control us?

» What happens when we allow our anger to control us?

» Apply this to yourself: In what situations have you been controlled by your anger and done something sinful and destructive rather than having been in control of your anger (James 1:20)?

» Write out one of the verses in this section that describes this controlling kind of anger:

_____

_____

_____

_____

Our anger is sinful when it becomes the dominant feature of our life. If other people's first impressions of us are that we are touchy, irritable, or easily annoyed, then we may have a problem with sinful anger. If we find that people seem to be constantly "tip-toeing" around us, it could be an indication that we have a chronic problem with sinful anger.

Proverbs 19:19 refers to a person of "great" anger: "A man of great anger will bear the penalty, for if you rescue him, you will only have to do it again." Proverbs 22:24 presents a similar idea when it says, "Do not associate with a man given to anger; or go with a hot-tempered man." These verses describe the type of people that we could call "anger addicts." They have turned the reins of their lives over to anger and are completely under its control. It's the norm—the pattern of their lives—for them to be angry.

In I Timothy 3:3, the Bible teaches that an elder of the church must not be "given to wine" (NKJV). In other words, he must not be addicted to alcohol. Drinking alcohol must not be the dominant feature of his life, such that he turns to it for satisfaction and relief from problems. The natural reaction for a person addicted to alcohol is to seek relief from life's pressures in it.

The two verses from Proverbs refer to the same idea; only the addiction is to anger. Anger is the immediate, natural response when the pressure is on. When this is true of someone, they're exhibiting sinful anger.

I have dear friends that I love to be around because they're sweet, easy to spend time with, and even-tempered. There are other people, however, who when I think about them, certain words immediately pop into my mind: "hostile," "angry," and "easily provoked." These people are very difficult to get along with and I don't enjoy spending time with them. If this kind of anger is characteristic of our lives, we need to recognize and deal with it because it's sinful anger.

APPLICATION QUESTIONS

»   What did the statement mean that anger is sinful when it becomes the dominant feature of a per son's life?

»   What happens when anger becomes a dominant feature of a person's life?

»   Have you personally dealt with your anger in this way? When? In what circumstances or situations?

» Write out one of the verses in this section that describes this kind of anger:

_____

_____

_____

_____

In summary, anger can be godly and constructive or it can be ungodly and destructive. When God expresses anger, it's always righteous. When we express our anger, it's often—if not usually—unrighteous. In our study of anger thus far, we have learned that anger that occurs for sinful reasons, such as jealousy, is sinful anger. Anger that controls us—causes us to act out of passion—is likewise sinful anger. And anger that is the dominant feature of our lives is sinful anger as well. There are several other characteristics of sinful anger, and we will continue to look at these in chapter two of this book.

1   See my study on anger in *A Homework Manual for Biblical Living,*
     Volume 1 (Phillipsburg: P&R Publishers, 1979), pp. 5-8

CHAPTER 2

WHEN IS ANGER WRONG?

Controlling anger is usually a life-long struggle. From the temper-tantrums of young children, to the moody sulking of teens, to the resentful bitterness of adults, sinful anger is generally a constant in our lives to some degree—changing forms, perhaps—but never overcome completely. Proverbs 14:29 teaches that it requires wisdom to control our anger. "He who is slow to anger has great understanding." In this chapter, we will learn several more characteristics of sinful anger. In the next chapters, we will consider what God's solution to our problem is.

I. Our anger is sinful when it involves brooding or fretting.

Brooding and fretting is a common reaction when something occurs that we did not want to happen or when something does not occur that we did want to happen. Psalm 37 could be called the "Fretter's Psalm." Three times in the first eight verses of this psalm, God says, "Fret not." Verses one and seven describe circumstances in which we are prone to fret—when evil men do evil things, and verse eight gives us a reason why we should not fret. It says, "Cease from anger and forsake wrath; do not fret; *it leads only to evil doing.*"

"Fret" is not a word we use much anymore, but it means to constantly think through distressing events in one's mind while giving those events a negative slant. To put it in the words of Proverbs 30:33, fretting involves churning your displeasure into anger in the same way that milk is churned into butter. It means constantly dwelling on some personal slight, until what started as a small annoyance is built up into an enormous offense.

In other words, if we were to think of our minds as a stereo, churning our anger means that, in our minds, we are playing the recording of this offense—what someone did or said to us that angered us—over and over and over again. And every time we play it over in our minds, the recording gets a little louder and a little stronger. Eventually, that one recording is ingrained in our minds to the point that it plays by itself, without deliberate thought. At the end of Proverbs 30:33, God says, "...so the churning of anger produces strife." He is warning us that churning our anger, or fretting, only leads to sin and more conflict.

The teaching of these verses in the Psalms and Proverbs parallels the teaching in Ephesians 4:26-27. God says, "Do not let the sun go down on your anger, and do not give the devil an opportunity." In other words, we are commanded not to carry our troubles from one day into the next. Satan loves to see us stew over the wrongs that we have had done to us, but God wants us to put them behind us so that we are not tempted to sin.

Indeed, I have had men in my counseling room that were still brooding and fretting over something that their wives did to them two or three decades ago! This event continued to be a source of irritation to them, not days, but years later. They had never given up their anger, and it was actively eroding their marriage as much in the present as when it first occurred. These men were doing what Proverbs 30:33 condemns: churning their anger into strife. Many people who have been offended or hurt by someone will do this kind of churning and fretting. Like all sin, over time it begins to control their thinking. God says that this is sinful anger.

A P P L I C A T I O N   Q U E S T I O N S

>> What was meant by the statement that sinful anger is characterized by the practice of brooding or fretting?

>> What happens when we brood or fret over what does or does not happen to us?

>> Have you personally dealt with your anger in this way? When? In what circumstances or situations?

>> Write out one of the verses in this section that describes this kind of anger:

_____

_____

_____

_____

II. Our anger is sinful when we keep a running record of how we have been mistreated.

I Corinthians 13:5 says that love does not keep a record of wrongs that have been done to it. Some time ago, a husband and wife came to me for counseling. They had been separated for a period of time and were now trying to put their marriage back together. As is usually the case, the husband was very ready to tell me about the wrongs that his wife had done, and the wife was eager to tell me about the wrongs that her husband had done. In fact, this woman said to me, "If you want, next week I'll bring in my notebook. I've kept a daily record for the last three years of the wrongs that my husband has done to me." Imagine that!

No wonder this woman had bitterness and resentment toward her husband! No wonder the marriage was breaking down! Every day she recorded all the wrong things that her husband had done. She reviewed her list during her daily devotions, which were in the same notebook. She thought that she had built up a good case against her husband and his sinfulness. Needless to say, what that woman was doing was wrong. We are harboring sinful anger whenever we become resentful or bear a grudge.

In Leviticus 19:18, the Bible says, "You shall not...bear any grudge against the sons of your people, but you shall love your neighbor as yourself." In Mark 6, as we noted earlier, Herodias "had it in" for John the Baptist. She had a grudge against him because of what he had said about her lifestyle. In her heart, there was resentment and anger that she never forgot. Bearing a grudge against another person, whoever it may be, is sinful anger.

Keeping a record of wrongs leads quickly to bitterness. Hebrews 12:15 speaks of a "root of bitterness." In other words, this type of anger is not a simple, surface matter. It becomes a root in our lives, deeply ingrained. The Scripture warns us that if this root is in us, it could cause "many [to] be defiled." We will defile ourselves and we will defile others as well by our bitter anger.

I have seen parents whose bitterness against other people has been a destructive example to their children. Their bitterness allowed the devil to gain a foothold in their children's lives. Sadly, parents can pass their bitterness on to their children. We who are parents ought to check our own lives carefully if we find that our children are becoming grudge-holders. Our own attitudes—both good and bad—are models for our children.

A poor example or a serious provocation is not an excuse, however, for becoming bitter. I counseled a man whose wife had left him and who had every reason—by the world's standards—to be bitter towards his wife. After she left him, she deliberately did things to humiliate and anger him. She ran around with another man, going to places that she knew her husband would be. She gave him every opportunity to resent her.

This man had to deal with some tremendous provocations to anger. He acknowledged that there were times when he really wanted to deal with this other man and with his wife in a nasty way. By the grace of God, he was able to control himself. Nevertheless, I admonished him to be very careful that bitterness and resentment not be allowed to grow in his heart. I warned him that God would not allow him to hold grudges against his wife or the other man (Ephesians 4:31). If he did, not only would he displease God and harm himself, but his children would be affected and injured as well.

The Bible seems to indicate that bitterness is a special problem for husbands. In Colossians 3:19, it says, "Husbands, love your wives and do not be embittered against them." It can be easy for a man to become embittered against his wife for many reasons: she may not cooperate with him at times, she may not express affection as he prefers, she may not spend money the way he would like her to, she may not come to him for advice or follow his counsel, she may not support his ideas about handling certain situations, she may not be as excited about the things that excite him as he would like her to be, she may contradict him before the children or in the presence of other people, or she may not follow through on doing the things he has asked her to do. God knows that it's easy for a man to allow himself to become embittered for these reasons and many more. So He expressly warns men against this sin. He gave this command in the context of family relationships because a man's bitterness will affect not only himself, but his wife and his children also.

There are many bitter, resentful people in the world. The Bible says, *"Let all bitterness...be put away from you, along with all malice"* (Ephesians 4:31). We are clearly commanded to put aside all bitterness, regardless of the source. This means that keeping a record of wrongs, a practice that always produces bitterness, is a characteristic of sinful anger.

APPLICATION QUESTIONS

> » What was meant by the statement that sinful anger is connected to keeping a record of wrongs?
> » What happens when we keep a record of wrongs?
> » Have you personally dealt with your anger in this way? When? In what circumstances or situations?
> » Write out one of the verses in this section that describes this kind of anger:

_____

_____

_____

_____

III. Our anger is sinful when we pretend that we are not angry.

Ephesians 4:25 says, "Therefore, laying aside falsehood, speak truth each one of you with his neighbor." James 5:16 admonishes, "Therefore, confess your sins to one another." How often we are liars in this matter of anger! Our spouse or friend comes to us and says, "Is something wrong? Are you upset with me?" and we lie, "No, I'm fine. Nothing's wrong."

Many times, I have said to husbands or wives that I'm counseling, "You are an angry person. You are filled with bitterness against your spouse." They respond: "Me? I'm not angry! I'm not bitter!" Even as they say the words, their faces become red and their fists clench. Some of them have almost pounded on my desk and declared, "I'm not angry!" They lie about their anger, and then they wonder why they have ulcers, heart palpitations, high blood pressure, and other physical problems. They wonder why they so easily lose their cool. Worse yet, they cannot figure out why they no longer get anything out of the Word of God, why their pastor's messages no longer speak to them, and why their prayer lives are so ineffective.

For example, consider a woman who has come in for counseling. She claims to have an abusive husband and says that she is afraid of him. "He has an explosive temper," she says. To prevent her from going on and on about her husband in a general, disparaging, unwholesome and unhelpful way that will neither help her nor the situation, I make an attempt to direct the conversation to something that will be more constructive. I tell her that I understand that she has been hurt by what she has experienced and that I'm here to help her find God's help for handling a very difficult situation. I remind her that God is able to make all grace abound to her so that she, having all sufficiency in all things, might abound unto every good work (2 Corinthians 9:8).

I refer to the fact God will be faithful to her in whatever situation she finds herself and that He has promised to make a way of escape so that she will be able to bear it (I Corinthians 10:13). I inform her that I want to help her find that way of escape and that to do so I will want to ask some questions. I make it as clear as possible that I would like her to be as concise and factual as possible in the answers she gives, and that my purpose for asking her these several questions is to gain information so that I might be able guide her in constructively handling the pressures she is facing.

I then ask her to describe as factually as possible some specific examples of instances when she has been mistreated. "Please give me a description of what happened. Where did it happen? When did it happen? What did you do before it happened? How did you respond when it happened? Describe your verbal and behavioral response. What did you actually say? What did you actually do?"

Over a period of time, as I counsel her, I discover that she is not responding in a biblically constructive way. I know that her husband was responsible before God for what he did to provoke the problem, but I also know that she is responsible before God for prolonging the problem by her unbiblical response. There are some people who provoke trouble, and there are others who prolong trouble. In either case, whether a person is a provoker or a prolonger, that person is sinning.

We've all heard the saying, "Two wrongs don't make a right." The Bible says, "All of you be harmonious...and humble in spirit; *not returning evil for evil or insult for insult*, but giving a blessing instead" (I Peter 3:8-9). If someone sins against us, he is wrong; but if we respond sinfully, we are wrong as well. The other person's sin does not excuse our own. In our example, this woman is sinning in her response to her husband's sins against her. She claims to not be angry with him, but her bitter and complaining words give away the truth.

I make it clear to her that if her husband did, and is doing, what she described, he was sinning against her. I flat out tell her he has no justification for treating her the way she says he has; I indicate that being treated the way she described would be a great trial. I do everything I can to be as gentle and non-condemning as I can. Then, I gently and tactfully ask her to tell me how she thinks God would have her respond to that kind of treatment. I ask her if she can think of any Bible verses that might provide direction for her in a situation like this. When she can't think of any, I suggest that we turn to several passages of Scripture that provide relevant guidance. We turn to such passages as Proverbs 15:1, 18; Ephesians 4:29-31; Romans 12:14-21; and Colossians 4:6. Then we carefully talk about what God would say about the biblical way of handling difficult situations. At that point, in spite of the careful way I have tried to avoid being heavy handed or coming across in an insensitive way, she immediately responds, "You don't live where I live! You don't understand my situation! You're not experiencing what I'm experiencing! You're saying that I'm wrong. You're saying it's my entire fault! I'm not the one who is doing wrong in this situation. My husband is the only one who is responsible for this mess." She refuses to acknowledge that she has done anything wrong and that there is any way in which she needs to change.

Then having released her anger, she gets up and storms out of my office. What did she do? With her words and her actions, she gave me a perfect example of how she had most likely behaved with her husband. She is a bitter, angry woman, but she refuses to admit it. Sadly, she will never solve her own problem, or do God's will to solve the problems in her marriage, until she stops shifting all the blame to her husband. She will never make any progress until she can say, "My husband is wrong in what he's doing. He is responsible for any of his attitudes and behaviors that are unbiblical, but as Matthew 7:2-5 states, I'm responsible for my attitudes and behavior also, and I need to first acknowledge and deal with what is unbiblical in my own life. And, with God's help, I can bear what is coming my way and find a way of escape. By God's grace I can learn to return good for evil; I can refrain from reviling when I'm reviled, from insulting when I'm insulted. I can learn to bless when I'm cursed" (Romans 12:21; I Peter 2:8-13).

We are handling our anger sinfully whenever we justify our bitterness and resentment or when we pretend that we are not angry. In my life, when I find myself getting angry, I have found it very helpful to say, "Wayne, you are getting angry and your anger is your responsibility, not someone else's. No one can crawl in you and make you angry. All they can do is provide the context in which you become angry. Wayne, if you become angry, you get all the credit for that anger. Your anger is coming from inside you, not from the outside."

To control my anger, I must recognize and acknowledge its presence and not play justification or denial games. I must put away lying and speak the truth to myself, refusing to use euphemisms that tend to lessen the seriousness of my anger. I must recognize that though there are degrees of anger, every instance of anger that is connected to the things we have mentioned in this chapter is a variation of the same emotion and that every instance stems from the same root. In degree, one experience of anger may be different from another, but in kind they're all the same. In other words, I must recognize that to be hurt or upset or slightly annoyed is only different in degree from being furious or enraged. I must understand that whether I'm slightly annoyed or infuriated, I'm handling the pressures of life in an ungodly way. Having done that, I find it helpful to go on to say, "Lord, you already know that I'm angry for the wrong reasons (some of which have been mentioned in this chapter) and being tempted to respond to it and express it in ungodly ways. I'm confessing this to you and to myself. I take full responsibility. Please forgive me and please help me to understand what would be a godly response, and then help me to actually respond in a biblically constructive way."

» What was meant by the statement that sinful anger is characterized by denial?

» What happens when we deny our anger?

» Have you personally dealt with your anger in this way? When? In what circumstances or situations?

» Write out one of the verses in this section that describes this kind of anger:

_____

_____

_____

_____

IV. Our anger is sinful when we return evil for evil or attack the person with whom we are angry.

When Cain attacked and killed his brother Abel in Genesis 4, he committed this sin. Proverbs 29:11 says, "A fool always loses his temper." Proverbs 29:22 adds, "And a hot-tempered man abounds in transgression." Proverbs 12:16 states: "A fool's anger is known at once." When this kind of person is angry, everyone knows it immediately because he or she cannot contain their anger. They give vent to their anger as soon as they feel it and they do it in one of three ways.

One, they express their anger *verbally*. In I Samuel 20, Saul did this to his son Jonathan. The Bible says, "Then Saul's anger burned against Jonathan and he said to him, 'You son of a perverse, rebellious woman! Do I not know that you are choosing the son of Jesse to your own shame...'?" (20:30). Certainly, this was not a very nice thing to say to his own son. Saul was known for having a very short fuse and a violent temper.

Some children become very good at expressing their anger this way. Perhaps, if they're bigger than everyone else is, then they will bully others verbally when they're angry just because they can. Or, maybe they're smaller than everyone else is, and so they use angry words to make themselves seem as big and strong as they would like to be. Big or small, these children learn sinful patterns of response to their anger. They learn that when they yell louder than their parents, siblings, or classmates, they get their way. As adults, the pattern is ingrained, and they're still exploding verbally at others.

Two, some people express their anger *passively*. This seems to be especially true of women, who often realize that they will not get their way by yelling louder. Their parents can always yell louder than they can, so little girls, and sometimes boys as well, learn to retreat. They go to their rooms, pouting and stewing. Their complete lack of a verbal response is actually an expression of their anger. As adults, they retreat into silence whenever they're upset. They refuse to talk, shutting the offending person out, "punishing" them by ignoring them. Their silence is a form of passive revenge for the hurt that they have experienced.

Three, some people express their anger *physically*. When they're angry, they shove, kick, push, bite and scratch. These days, we often hear about women who are physically abused by their husbands. I find that this is a problem in many cases when I counsel people about marriage problems. However, I have seen a number of cases where a wife has physically abused her husband. In fact, not long ago, a physician came into my office and said, "I'm afraid to stay in my home. The other night, I was taking a nap on my bed and my wife came in with her big pocketbook and whacked me with it!" This man told me that his wife had thrown lamps and plates at him. He was literally afraid for his life, and both of them claimed to be Christians.

As we all know, physical abuse in families is not just confined to husbands and wives. Parents sometimes abuse their children, and in recent years, there has been a significant increase in cases of children acting out their anger physically toward their parents. Parents have been shot and killed by their own children. Sadly, this type of thing goes on even in the homes of some professing Christians.

Vengeful anger is a dangerous, destructive sin no matter how it is expressed towards others. Several years ago, a young man came to me for counseling who was what a secular psychiatrist would have diagnosed as "paranoid-schizophrenic." He seemed to be afraid of everything and had a glassy stare and strange mannerisms. He told me that he had regularly sniffed gasoline years ago. Through our counseling sessions, however, I discovered something much more significant.

As a young boy, other kids had frequently picked on this man because of his small size. This caused his mind to be dominated by fear. In his estimation, everyone was mocking him. Everyone was his enemy, and bitterness and resentment began to grow in his heart toward everyone and everything. Eventually, it affected the way he perceived complete strangers. Because of his childhood fear, he imagined that everyone was out to get him.

One day, he came into my office and told me that he had cast death spells on his old high school classmates. What was this young man doing? In his own way, he was expressing his sinful anger. He was avenging the wrong that he felt had been done to him. We may not go to such extremes, but whenever we lash out verbally, passively, or physically against others, we are handling our anger in a sinful way.

APPLICATION QUESTIONS

» What did the statement mean that our anger is sinful when we return evil for evil or attack the person with whom we are angry?

» Give some biblical or contemporary examples of this kind of sinful anger.

» Give some examples of times when you have personally expressed your anger in this way.

» What happens when we express our anger in this way?

» Write out one of the verses in this section that describes this kind of anger:

_____

_____

_____

_____

V. Our anger is sinful when we attack or hurt a substitute.

I believe that was what Saul did to Jonathan in I Samuel 20. Saul was really angry with David, not Jonathan, but he took it out on his son because he was closer. I believe that was what Moses did in Exodus 32, when he saw the sin of the Israelites. He became angry and smashed the tablets of stone that God had just given to him. I believe that was also what Moses did in Numbers 20 when he struck the rock. Moses was angry with the people for grumbling and complaining, so he took his anger out on the rock as a substitute. It was sinful anger, and God punished Moses for it by not allowing him to enter the Promised Land.

A couple came to me for counseling because the husband had been hitting his wife. Through our time together, I discovered that this man was harboring a great deal of resentment against his mother. His mother had been the dominant figure in his home. She had run his father's life, and she had run his life. More than that, he believed that his mother had rejected him because, among other things, she sent him to live with his grandmother for long periods of time. This caused him to think that he was a bother to her.

He carried this deep, bitter resentment of his mother into his marriage. When his wife did something that reminded him of his mother—when she seemed to be bossy and domineering—he would often punch her in the mouth. His reaction was not only an angry response to his wife, but in a sense, to his mother as well. The anger that he expressed for his wife was in some ways a substitute for the anger that he wanted to express for his mother.

A similar example would be a man who, when he has a problem at work with his boss, comes home and takes it out on his family. He yells at his wife, or is nasty with his children, or kicks the dog. If he had not already been upset with his boss, whatever his wife or children did or did not do would not have upset him as much, or perhaps at all. He really attacked them as a substitute for his boss.

Some secular psychologists and psychiatrists encourage a practice that is called "venting." If they have a client who is angry or resentful toward someone else—perhaps their mother or father—they might hand them a pillow and encourage their client to do to the pillow what they would like to do to the person with whom they're upset. If their client makes a half-hearted go of it, they encourage them, "You're angrier than that! Hit harder! Let your anger out!" They cheer their client on in their rage to the point that they lose control and beat the pillow to rags.

This may be a recommended method of dealing with anger, but in fact, it leads only to sin, not a solution to the problem. The Word of God says, "You have heard that the ancients were told, 'You shall not commit murder' and 'Whoever commits murder shall be liable to the court.' But I say to you that everyone who is angry with his brother shall be guilty before the court" (Matthew 5:21-22). Abusing another person in our hearts and minds is just as sinful and wrong as far as God is concerned as is abusing them physically.

Another practice among secular psychologists and psychiatrists— and even some Christian ones—is something called "transference."

In this method of dealing with anger, the counselor will try to take the place of the person with which their client is upset. The counselor might say, "Pretend that I'm your mom and tell me everything that you would like to tell her. Let me really have it!" Again, what the counselor is doing is encouraging their client to attack a substitute. I'm convinced that this is a sinful expression of anger. God never encourages us to attack a substitute, or to "transfer" our anger to another person, or to "vent" our anger on something else. As we saw in the examples from Scripture, God punished this kind of thing in his servant Moses' life.

APPLICATION QUESTIONS

>> What was meant by the statement that sinful anger is characterized by attacking a substitute?
>> What happens when we attack a substitute?
>> Have you personally dealt with your anger in this way? When? In what circumstances or situations?
>> What biblical examples of this kind of anger were found in this section?

All of the types of anger that we have studied in this and the previous chapter are sinful expressions of anger. They're all a part of the anger, bitterness, and wrath that Ephesians 4:31 says we must put off. They're all sinful, God-dishonoring, and people-destroying ways of responding to the pressures and problems of life. As such, God wants us to expunge them from our lives.

In order to do this, we must first carefully consider which types of anger we are most prone to express. Before continuing to the next chapter, go back over your answers to the application questions and summarize what you have learned about the kinds of anger that need to be put off. Acknowledge your sinful propensities to God, to family members, and to close friends. Ask God and others whom you have wronged for forgiveness. Seek His help and the help of the people to whom you have acknowledged your sin. Commit yourself to learning a new, godly way of responding to the pressures and problems of life.

Complete the concluding application exercise that follows this paragraph. In the next two chapters we will present important principles for learning how to be good and angry. In other words, we will present practical information on how to make anger a constructive force in your life and experience.

CONCLUDING APPLICATION EXERCISE

» Write out your summary of the most important truths about sinful anger that was presented in this chapter.

_____

_____

_____

_____

» Are you or any of your family members guilty of any of the forms of sinful anger described in this chapter? Begin by evaluating yourself. Specifically identify the ways in which you have been guilty (Matthew 7:2-5). Then go on to evaluate other family members (Galatians 6:1-2).

_____

_____

_____

_____

» What will you do to change these sinful responses?

_____

_____

_____

_____

» How can you help other family members to overcome their sinful anger patterns?

_____

_____

_____

_____

CHAPTER 3

LEARNING TO BE GOOD AND ANGRY

Most of us have been "good and angry" in a bad sense, meaning that we have been angry for the wrong reasons and expressed that anger in unbiblical ways, at some point in our lives. Something has happened, or someone has said something, that has really gotten us steamed. In fact, that reaction—becoming "good (or should I say, bad) and angry"—was as natural and easy for us as breathing. No one had to teach us how to get that angry. Our sinful hearts were all too eager to lead us into it.

There are far fewer of us that can claim to have ever been really good (in a godly sense) and angry, in other words, angry without sin, angry for the right reasons as well as expressing that anger in constructive, biblical ways.

In the last two chapters, we studied the different characteristics of sinful anger and the many ways that it can be expressed. This kind of anger comes naturally to us as sinners. What does not come naturally is dealing with our anger in a God-honoring way. This is something that we need to learn and train our hearts to do. In this chapter, we are going to look at what the Scripture says about being good and angry—dealing with our anger in a godly way.

The first aspect of learning to be good and angry is *dealing with problems on a regular, daily basis*. Ephesians 4:26-27 says, "Be angry, and yet do not sin; do not let the sun go down on your anger." In this verse, God has commanded us to deal with our problems *every day*. What often happens when there is a problem between people is that they not only allow the sun to go down on it, but they allow many moons to go down as well. Years later, they're still bothered by things that were never taken care of when they first happened. Over time, other things have been added to the original offense, and now they're harboring a mountain of anger in their hearts.

I remember a counseling occasion in which a man actually said that he was going to leave his wife because "she didn't close the dresser drawers." He complained that he would come into his bedroom, step around a corner, and get a stomach full of open drawers. The truth, of course, was that this man had more than a stomach full of drawers; he had a stomach full of his wife as well. He was upset about the drawers plus a thousand other things that had accumulated over the years. The drawers had simply become the focal point of his growing anger.

Whenever we see a person responding with an unusual amount of emotion and anger to what most people would consider a miniscule thing, we can be sure that person has had much unexpressed anger, simmering under the surface, from prior events. This person's response to that one problem was really a reaction to that and many other things that he has not yet dealt with because he was not resolving his anger on a regular basis.

According to God's Word, there are only two ways to deal righteously with a conflict that we have with another person. One, we can overlook the offense. I Peter 4:8 says "love covers a multitude of sins." Proverbs 10:12 teaches, "Hatred stirs up strife, but love covers all transgressions." Proverbs 19:11 says, "A man's discretion makes him slow to anger, and *it is his glory to overlook a transgression.*"

Some people might think that it's their duty to point out other people's sins to them. After all, they opine that the Bible teaches us to confront sin in others (II Thessalonians 3:14-15). Though the Scripture does teach this, it's also true that Scripture tells us to overlook some sin. There are times, as Proverbs 19:11 indicates, when it's better for us to overlook an offense than to point it out. If a person is doing something that does not greatly hinder his ministry or someone else's ministry for Jesus Christ or that does not hurt someone else or that is not a pattern in that person's life, it may be better to overlook it, praying that the other person would be convicted by the Holy Spirit. It's generally better to reserve confrontation for spiritual issues that are clearly sin issues, issues that will bring reproach on Christ and serious damage to other people. In other words, we need to distinguish between what we could call swing issues and fire issues. Fire issues destroy and maim; they do serious damage. Swing issues are of less consequence. We certainly need to distinguish between preference and sin issues, between what is really major and what is relatively minor.

For example, my children were born with sinful hearts that are "more deceitful than all else and [are] desperately sick" (Jeremiah 17:9). If I had wanted to, I could have observed the lives of my children as they were growing up and found almost innumerable things wrong with what they said and did. In fact, I could have occupied a large part of my day just in rebuking and criticizing them—pointing out their sins.

After a while, however, they would have begun to think of me as a policeman, not a father. My relationship with them would have suffered greatly as a result. My positive impact on them for good would have been hindered as they encountered my constant negativity. Continuous, non-stop faultfinding and admonition would have encouraged them to be uptight around me and to want to avoid me as much as possible.

What we should do as parents, or spouses, or friends, is overlook the things which do not fit the categories I've just mentioned and confront people about the things that are of vital importance as outlined previously. We need to choose our battles carefully and wisely. In the book, *Life in the Father's House*, a book I coauthored, we make this statement:

> We should confront someone only when he or she acts in a way forbidden in Scripture. That means being careful not to confront another based on mere preference outside of Scripture (I Cor. 4:6) or even a principle inferred from Scripture by "exegetical gymnastics" and wrongly elevated to a universal standard (cf. Romans 14:1-12).... The Scriptures speak to many issues clearly, and those explicit principles are a sufficient basis for reproof and correction (2 Tim. 3:16). In matters outside the clear teaching of Scripture, each person should be "fully convinced in his own mind" (Rom. 14:5) but should

also be very careful not to judge his brother (Rom. 14:4, 10, 13).

If we took the time to confront every possible sin that other Christians commit we would probably have little time for anything else. Inconsiderate words and actions, selfish oversights, and prideful thoughts expressed in some way are rampant in any body of believers and in family relationships. Many of those offenses do not need to be discussed, but can be overlooked.

Growing in biblical love and humility will help you to cover more and more offenses (especially those committed against you), and growing in biblical wisdom can help you to decide what sins should not be overlooked because of their harmful consequences.

A question you should ask yourself is this: ... would one or two more people of sound judgment consider this issue significant enough to go along with me? If not, then perhaps the problem should be overlooked at this time.

If you seriously question whether to confront someone or not, perhaps it would be better to be safe than sorry. Perhaps you should lovingly ask the person about the issue. But as we grow in our love and humility towards others in the body, we should increasingly learn to overlook a multitude of offenses recognizing that we must gratefully thank others for covering our sins as well.[1]

What you have just read suggests that there is a second way of dealing with a conflict that we have with another person. When we experience or recognize a serious problem with another person because of their sin, then, as Matthew 18:15 says, we are to go privately to that person for the purpose of resolving the problem. The purpose of that meeting should be only for promoting reconciliation and unity, not for criticizing or condemning.

For example, if we have a conflict with another person over what may be a relatively small thing and we have made an effort to overlook the offense, but this same conflict recurs frequently, then it would be sin to keep quiet about the matter. Or, if we have a conflict with another person that, even though it only happens once, is of very serious consequence, then it also would be sin for us to keep quiet.

These principles should be applied in our relationships with friends or colleagues and they should also be implemented in our marriage relationships. In a Christian marriage, our spouse is a fellow brother or sister in Christ and deserves the same treatment as any other person. God's Word commands us to deal with our serious conflicts by going to the other person and discussing the matter, for the purpose of reconciliation.

In *Life in the Father's House*, we make this comment:

> Love covers a multitude of sins, but sometimes sin throws the cover off. When the following conditions exist, it becomes unloving and wrong to ignore the problem: If the sin creates an unreconciled relationship between you and the offender, so that you think often about the sin and think badly of him, then confrontation is necessary for the sake of unity in the body (of Matt. 5:23,24; Phil. 2:1-4).
>
> If you are not confident that the person is growing in the direction of Christlikeness by regularly confessing his sin and working to change, then confronting his sin may be the only way to expose his spiritual inertia and help him avoid God's chastening (of Heb. 3:12-14; James 5:19,20; 2 Peter 1:5-10).
>
> If you know that there will be consequences of this sin that will hurt others in the offender's life, then for their sake you should make sure that he has recognized his wrong and repented from it (of Matt. 18:15-16; I Cor. 5:6-7; 12:26).[2]

One practical way to ensure that problems are dealt with on a regular basis is by establishing a daily family conference time. This is a designated time in every day in which the family discusses things together. The amount of time set apart for this may be short or long, depending on what problematic issues are happening in the family at the time. In my marriage relationship, even when I'm traveling for a seminar or other teaching commitment, I do my best to call my wife every day or, if for some reason that is very difficult, I contact her at least every two days. I do this because I want to maintain contact, but I also want to know about anything that has developed—any problems— in our family. I cannot be the head of our home unless I know what is happening there. I cannot encourage and help my wife unless I talk to her regularly.

Setting aside *a specific time* during each day to deal with problems can be a very beneficial practice. Doing this on a daily basis can accomplish two things: one, it can prevent the pile up of problems which will make it more difficult to resolve those problems when eventually they can't be ignored any longer; and two, having a specific time for the discussion of problems can prevent the practice of talking about problems continually throughout the day. It's usually not very productive to relationships if the whole day takes on the flavor of a problem. Having a specific time can be used to encourage children (and to remind ourselves) to consider things carefully before reacting. It's important for us to train ourselves to take stock of a situation, evaluate it carefully in light of Scripture, pray about it, and then decide what to do. Knee-jerk reactions to conflict are seldom, if ever, beneficial to anyone involved.

Indeed, we usually get into more trouble when our response is to "shoot from the hip." When we react without thinking first, we often compound the problem because the other person is not ready to receive the correction, and we are not ready to give it in a loving manner. This is true for parents and children and for husbands and wives. A regular time that has been set aside for discussing disagreements and offenses allows every family member the necessary time to prayerfully consider a proper response. And, if there are not problematic issues to discuss during this pre-established conference time, the regular time gives the family an opportunity for regularly conversing on positive issues.

"Do not let the sun go down on your anger" (Ephesians 4:26). "Sufficient unto each day is the trouble thereof" (Matthew 6:34). In other words, Scripture admonishes us to get today's problems taken care of today, so there is room for tomorrow's problems tomorrow. If we make this a habit, we will reap the benefits throughout our lives in our families and in our marriages. It will allow us to start each day fresh, free of leftover anger and bitterness.

APPLICATION QUESTIONS

» What is the first aspect of learning to be good and angry presented in this chapter?

» What may we assume whenever we see a person responding with an unusual amount of emotion and anger to what most people would consider a miniscule thing?

» What are the two ways to deal righteously with a conflict that we have with another person?
» What Scriptures support these two approaches?
» What criteria should be used to determine which of these two approaches to use in a given situation?
» Explain one practical way to ensure that problems are dealt with on a regular basis.
» Write out one of the verses in this section that describes how to handle with our anger:

_____
_____
_____
_____

» Do you always, often, sometimes, seldom, never practice the biblical way of dealing with the offenses, sins and conflicts of other people? Ask your mate and/or children to evaluate how they think you should answer this question.

The second aspect of learning to be *good* and angry is *understanding that we can control and restrain the expression of our anger.* If we are Christians, we have the means to control the expression of our anger. Proverbs 29:11 says, "A fool always loses his temper, but a wise man holds it back." Proverbs 16:32 teaches that a wise man rules his spirit. Since we have Christ, and in Christ are "hidden all the treasures of wisdom and knowledge" (Colossians 2:3), we have the power to be that wise person. By the power of the indwelling Holy Spirit, we can control our anger.

In fact, we do it all the time—when we really want to. Consider this illustration. Suppose a mother has a particularly bad day. Her husband was a real grouch in the morning. Her children were about as disobedient and rebellious as they could possibly be, constantly interrupting her work. The washing machine broke down and the vacuum stopped working. Nothing she wanted to accomplish was getting done that day. By mid-afternoon, as she was ready to pull her hair out, her children had one more good fight. At that point, she "lost control" and started screaming and yelling.

Just then, in the middle of her fireworks, the telephone rang. She picked up the phone, said a cheerful, "Hello!" and spent the next several minutes talking very pleasantly with her pastor's wife. What happened? This woman controlled her "out of control" anger.

Or consider this example. Someone is at his place of employment. The boss comes into the office and, clearly having a bad day, criticizes him for everything he has done that day. Most of the criticism is undeserved, and this person spends the rest of his day contemplating how much he would like to defend himself and prove to the boss that his assessment was wrong or even to punch his boss in the nose. He doesn't do it, of course, because he is afraid of losing his job.

What did this person do? He controlled his anger. We can and we do control our anger when the motivation is great. When we fail to control our anger, it's because *we don't consider the stakes to be high enough.* In other words, we think we can get away with losing our temper and letting the shrapnel fly all over the place. We don't think we will lose anything (our godly image at church, our job, etc.) and so we let it all hang out. We allow our anger to be a destructive force. For some strange reason, the place where we are most likely to think that we can get away with it is with our mates and children.

We think somehow that assaulting and attacking family members will serve some good purpose. We forget about the truth of James 1:20 which says that "the wrath of man" never accomplishes anything good. We ignore the truth of Ecclesiastes 7:9 which reminds us "anger rests in the bosom of fools." Somehow, we think that blasting away at people or things is a wise thing to do and is going to do some good. It never does. It always does harm in the home and every other place. Yet we repeat the same practice over and over again. For some strange reason, we think we can get away with it in certain situations. However, there are other times and places where we realize the serious consequences, usually to us and our well being, and so in those situations we do control our anger.

In all places, and all times, we must recognize the fact that as Christians indwelt by the Holy Spirit we do have the power to control our anger. We must realize that when we fail, it's by choice. God has given us the power to obey Him in this matter of anger. How then, do we go about controlling our anger in a practical way? First, if we desire to obey God by controlling our anger, we must never excuse, justify, or rationalize our anger. Second, we must prepare ourselves to acknowledge and deal with it honestly.

The third aspect of learning to be good and angry is *taking time to examine the reasons for our anger.* Whenever we start to become angry, we should immediately stop what we're doing and think about what is happening. I often instruct my counselees to make up small cards to help them with this. When they're caught in a pattern of sinful response, from years and years of practice, they need to be jolted out of it. I ask them to write, "STOP" on one side of the card so that they can use that as a reminder when they find themselves falling into the old pattern.

When we take time to stop and think, we are able to evaluate the reasons for our anger. Are we getting angry because some "right" of ours is being denied? (See discussion of the "rights" issue in the first chapter on overcoming anger.) Or is it because we love God, His truth, and His righteousness? Are we really concerned about the kingdom of God and about advancing the cause of Jesus Christ in the situation? Scripture indicates that many times our angry responses are related to pride and selfishness; we become angry because we want our own way, we want to control people or the situation and we're not able to do it (Proverbs 13:10; James 4:1-3).

The bottom line reason for much of our sinful anger is related to the fact that we have an agenda and someone or something is standing in the way of our fulfilling that agenda. So taking the time to evaluate why we are becoming angry can be a helpful way of identifying our sinful, idolatrous motives and promoting conviction of sin and repentance.

APPLICATION QUESTIONS

» What are the third and fourth aspects of learning how to be good and angry?
» What is meant by the statement that we can control our anger when we want to?
» Explain why it's *important* to take the time to examine the reasons for our anger.
» What is often the bottom line reason for sinful anger?
» Describe a couple of instances when you have controlled your anger and a couple when your anger has controlled you. In the light of what was stated in this section about why people sometimes do and sometimes don't control their anger, evaluate why you controlled your anger on some occasions and why you didn't on the other occasions.

» Write out one of the verses in this section that describes this kind of anger.

_____

_____

_____

_____

» Do you always, often, sometimes, seldom, never practice the godly anger management strategies discussed in this section? Ask your mate and/or children to evaluate how they think you should answer this question.

The fourth aspect of learning to be good and angry is *learning to harness the energy created by our anger.* It has been medically proven and documented that when people become angry, physical changes take place in their bodies. According to researchers, anger stimulates the adrenal gland, which then releases a hormone (commonly called adrenaline) into the bloodstream. This hormone stimulates other glands in the body, which also release hormones into the bloodstream. One of these glands is the pancreas, which makes insulin. Insulin helps the body turn glucose (sugar) into chemical energy that the body can use for work. In other words, anger stimulates the body to prepare to use energy—to do something—and we can use that for either destructive or constructive purposes.

If we constantly suppress our anger and the energy it builds up, we will eventually destroy ourselves. Unreleased stress in the body has been linked to all kinds of physical problems. In his book, *None of These Diseases,*[3] physician Dr. S.I. McMillen gives numerous illustrations of the serious consequences that anger and other strong emotions can have on the body. This, of course, is in keeping with the many biblical statements about the beneficial consequences pleasant emotions can have on our physical well being and the numerous warnings about the debilitating effects of negative emotions on our bodies. "A tranquil heart is life to the body, but passion is rottenness to the bones" (Proverbs 14:30). "When the heart is sad, the spirit is broken" (Proverbs 15:13). "A joyful heart is good medicine, but a broken spirit dries up the bones" (Proverbs 17:22). "…a broken spirit who can bear" (Proverbs 18:14).

In section one of his book, *The Christian Counselor's Medical Desk*

Reference,[4] physician Dr. Robert Smith writes about some biblical principles for promoting good physical health. On pages three to twenty five, he quotes numerous Bible verses describing the principles of good health and the things it delineates as possible causes of bad health. To illustrate the effect that sinful emotions may have on our bodies, I will include a few random statements from various parts of the book that draw the possible connection between our emotions and poor health: "there are some specific effects of sin and disobedience on the body and health";[5] "responses to various circumstances may themselves produce symptoms of sickness";[6] "anger sends impulses to the intestine, stimulating ... cramping and spasm. The result is more pain...in sixty to eighty percent of patients, responses to problems of life have produced physical symptoms";[7] "some headaches are due to muscle soreness resulting from holding the body rigid when under the pressure of solving problems. If any number of unbiblical responses to those difficulties such as irritation, resentment, or sinful anger are added, the headache may become worse."[8] Throughout the book, Dr. Smith explains how the experience of sinful anger along with other sinful emotions can have a negative effect on our bodies. So, when we suppress our anger and fail to deal with it biblically, we run the risk of not only displeasing God, but also bringing upon ourselves all kinds of physical problems. Suppression of anger, therefore, is not the answer to the sinful anger problem.

Conversely, it's also true that just letting it all come out, "blowing our top," engaging in the practice that psychologists call ventilating is not the answer. Most importantly, ventilating is not the answer because God warns against this practice (Proverbs 29:11; 16:32; Ephesians 4:31; Ephesians 4:26-27). Still further, "blowing your top" is not the answer because doing so will destroy other people and our relationships with them. Eventually, we may find ourselves alone and thinking that no one cares about us anymore. And if we take time to think about why nobody cares, we will often find that it's because of the hostile way in which we have treated them. Instead of using the energy created by our anger to destroy people, we should use that energy in a constructive way in dealing with problems.

In the next chapter I will enlarge on this concept of making anger a positive force in your life and relationships, and describe a biblically consistent procedure for doing this very thing. Meanwhile, after reading this chapter and completing the previous application exercises, conclude your study of this chapter by answering the following questions:

APPLICATION QUESTIONS

» What is the fourth aspect of learning to be good and angry presented in this chapter?

» What does the statement about harnessing the energy created by our anger mean?

» What two wrong ways of handling our anger are discussed in this section?

» What are the consequences of handling our anger in either of these two ways?

» Choose one or two verses that deal with overcoming sinful anger mentioned in this section and write them out in the following space:

_____

_____

_____

_____

» Reflect over the material presented in this chapter and write out the principles (ideas, concepts) that you thought were the most important, helpful, encouraging and convicting ones.

_____

_____

_____

_____

» How will you use this material in your own life or in your ministry to others?

_____

_____

_____

_____

1   Wayne Mack and David Swavely, *Life in the Father's House* (Phillipsburg, NJ: P&R Publishing, 1996), pp. 39-40

2   Ibid., 139

3   S.I. McMillen, David E. Stern, *None Of These Diseases* (Grand Rapids: Revell Publishing, 3rd edition; 6/1/2000)

4   Dr. Robert Smith, *The Christian Counselor's Medical Desk Reference* (Stanley, NC: Timeless Texts, 2000)

5   Ibid., p. 17

6   Ibid., p. 41

7   Ibid., p. 44

8   Ibid., p. 298

CHAPTER 4

SIX QUESTIONS THAT CAN MAKE THE DIFFERENCE

In the last chapter we talked about the importance of harnessing the energy created by anger and making it a positive force in your life and relationships. We emphasized that for believers this can be done. Jesus did it, Paul did it, Nehemiah did it and so can you and I. According to the Bible, we can "be angry and sin not" (Ephesians 4:26). I closed the last chapter by stating that in the next chapter I would describe a biblically based procedure for helping you to be good and angry. Here are my suggestions for accomplishing this very thing. When we find ourselves becoming angry, we can turn that anger into a constructive rather than a destructive force by stopping and asking ourselves the following six questions:

First, "*What is happening?*" Assess the situation. We should accurately identify the occasion and the presence of our sinful anger. For example, consider again the man driving home to a house littered with toys and bikes. When he feels his anger building, he should stop and ask himself what is happening. "Things are not going the way that I wanted them to. There are toys on the lawn, bicycles in the driveway, and I'm letting it bother me."

Or consider the situation where someone has agreed to help you and you're counting on his help, but he fails to show up and never takes the time to call and tell you that he won't make it. You must do whatever you were planning to do and you can't do what you were going to do without his help. So you start to get annoyed. That's the circumstance. What should you do? Should you pretend you're not upset? Should you deny that it bothers you? No, in that to do this would be to lie to yourself and possibly to others as well. In keeping with Scripture, you should put away lying and speak truth to yourself and to the Lord (Ephesians 4:25). Be honest about what is going on; don't play games! Certainly, you should remember that it's a foolish thing to have your temper control you rather than your controlling it.

Scripture says you should hold your anger back (Proverbs 29:11). Certainly, you should reflect on the fact that a man who "has no control over his spirit is like a city that is broken into and without walls" (Proverbs 25:28) and that it's important for you to rule your spirit (Proverbs 16:32) rather than being ruled by your spirit. But to rule your spirit (your emotions) you must first admit to yourself and to God that you are being disturbed.

Second, go on to answer the following set of questions: *What are my thoughts about what is happening? Am I interpreting what is happening or not happening through a biblical grid or am I leaning to my own understanding? Am I bringing my every thought into captivity and making myself think the way God would have me think?* (Proverbs 3:5,6; Roman 12:2; 2 Corinthians 10:1-5; Philippians 4:8). Here are a few examples of typical unbiblical ways of interpreting situations that must be replaced with godly, biblical thoughts if you are to overcome sinful anger:

> "I deserve much more than I'm getting."
> "If she had only listened to me."
> "I'm going to be late and it's a horrible thing to be late."
> "I told her what I wanted and she's not cooperating. She is so selfish."
> "That person totally misrepresented what I said or did."
> "After all I've done, this is what I get."
> "I deserve the praise or recognition more than the person who got it does."

"No matter what I do, it's just not good enough."

"My husband is never satisfied."

"No one ever pays any attention to me."

"No one cares what happens to me."

"People are always taking advantage of me."

"I'm always the one who has to give in or do the dirty work."

"She never wants to do what I want to do. She always has to have her own way."

"I'm always thinking about how I can please him, but he never thinks about what would please me." Etc.

Third, answer this set of questions: "*What do I want that I'm not getting or what am I getting that I don't want? What compelling desires of mine are driving me, ruling me, demanding to be fulfilled? What compelling desires of mine are being thwarted? Am I being motivated by the love of God or the love of self? Am I being controlled by a desire to please and glorify God or a desire to please and glorify self? What desires of mine have become demands? What wants of mine have become must have, can't live without desires?*" (I Corinthians 10:31; 2 Corinthians 5:9; Philippians 1:20,21; Colossians 3:1-3; Matthew 6:33; Jeremiah 45:5).

Here are some typically unbiblical desires that must be replaced with godly, biblical desires if you are to overcome sinful anger:

"I must have respect."

"I must have recognition."

"I must be happy."

"I must have a life that is free from pain and difficulty."

"I must have my own way and I'm not getting it."

"I must have people do what I want them to."

"I must be safe and secure."

"I must be as important as ..." "I must be the best and be treated as though I were the best." " I must have people praise me."

"I must succeed."

"I deserve to have a life that is free from criticism or opposition."

"I must have people think I'm intelligent and witty."

"I must have people agree with me or else I'm a failure."

"I must have children that ..."

"I must have a mate who ..."

Fourth, having answered this set of questions, go onto answer the question: *"Right now, what am I being tempted to do?"* Here are some very typical ways that people are tempted to, and actually do, respond when things don't go the way they want them to, or when they don't get what they think they must have or deserve:

"When I don't get what I want or think I must have, I'm tempted to lash out, to yell, to withdraw, to give someone a piece of my mind."
"I'm tempted to pout and sulk."
"I'm tempted to run away or quit."
"I'm tempted to brood and fret and nurse my wounds."
"I'm tempted to be irritable and let someone know I'm annoyed."
"I'm tempted to be malicious and hurt someone."
"I'm tempted to take drugs or turn to alcohol."
"I'm tempted to be stubborn and uncooperative."
"I'm tempted to punish or dominate someone who is standing in my way or who is not agreeing with me or not cooperating."
"I'm tempted to get revenge, to retaliate, to render railing for railing, accusation for accusation, insult for insult."
"I'm tempted to be pushy and overbearing. I'm tempted to be bitter and hold a grudge."

Fifth, In order to rule your emotions and respond in a godly way when things don't go the way you would like, it's crucial for you to answer the questions: *"How do my thoughts and intentions and potential response to the circumstances I'm confronting line up with Scripture? What would be the biblical, God-honoring response to this situation? How would God want me to think about and respond to this situation? What would be a Scriptural, godly, Christlike way of reacting to what is occurring?"* To overcome sinful anger, you must determine what would be the godly response. Study the Scripture and memorize and meditate on verses that delineate a biblical, constructive response to what could be an anger facilitating circumstance. Think carefully about the kind of response that would please God.

Remember, we are transformed by the renewing of our minds (Romans 12:2; Ephesians 4:23), and that the right use of Scripture will keep us from sin (Psalm 119:9,11). Fill your mind with relevant Scriptural thoughts about the way you should respond to what is happening. Here are a few examples of what you might do to develop a biblical response to undesirable, unpleasant, difficult circumstances.

When confronted by unpleasant, potentially irritating circumstances, you might stop and say to yourself: "God says that I'm to always act in a loving manner (John 13:34-35; 1 Corinthians 13:4-8; I Corinthians 16:14). What is love? Well, Scripture says that love is longsuffering and kind. Love isn't jealous or proud. Love isn't provoked. Love doesn't vaunt itself; it doesn't act unbecomingly; it doesn't seek its own; it doesn't take account of a wrong suffered. Love bears all things, believes all things, hopes all things. God says, 'The fruit of the Spirit is love' (Galatians 5:22). So I must purpose to love in the way God wants me to love and ask Him for help to do so. What would be the loving thing to do in this situation? How can I show my love for God and others at this time?"

Furthermore you might say to yourself, "God wants me to be wise in the way I handle what is happening. Scripture says, 'A wise man is slow to anger and it is his glory to pass by transgression' (Proverbs 19:11). God's Word tells me that I should let His word dwell in me richly, and that I should ask Him for insight and understanding so that I might have wisdom and act wisely, rather than sinfully and foolishly (Colossians 3:16; James. 1:5; Proverbs 2:1-5; Ephesians 5:15-17). So I must think through the truths presented in these passages about how to handle opposition and difficulties, and I must seek God's help to respond to them in a biblical way. I must stop and ask, what is the wise thing to do in this situation? How can I avoid doing what is foolish and make the most out of an undesirable situation?"

From there, you might proceed to remind yourself of the following biblical truths. You might remind yourself that God says, "The servant of the Lord must not strive, but be gentle" (2 Timothy 2:24-25). You might meditate on the fact that God's Word admonishes us to walk worthy of the calling with which we have been called with all humility, all patience, all gentleness and forbearance (Ephesians 4:1-2). You might call to mind the Scriptural exhortation about being forbearing with all men and at all times (Philippians 4:5). You might find help in reflecting on the biblical command about blessing when you are cursed, about returning good for evil, about counting it all joy when you encounter various kinds of trials (Matthew 5:43; 1 Peter 3:9-12; Romans 12:17-21; James 1:2-4).

Then, having filled your mind with God's perspectives, you should purpose to respond to what is happening in the way described in these verses and ask God for help to actually do this. You should ask yourself, what would be the gentle, humble, forbearing way of responding to what I'm experiencing? What would be the returning good for evil approach to this situation? What would be the God-honoring way of handling what has occurred?

Sixth, Finally, you should ask yourself: *"What will I choose to do at this time? Will I choose to obey God or self? Will I do God's will and please Him or will I do my will and please myself?"* Scripture makes it clear that if you're a real Christian you don't need to continue to respond to your difficulties in an angry, sinful or destructive manner. For those of us who are in Christ, sin is no longer our master and lord. We don't have to let sin reign in our mortal bodies that we should obey its lusts (desires). We have been freed from the controlling power of sin and have become slaves of righteousness (Romans 6:12-20). We are now able to put off the old man and put on the new man with godly ways of living and handling the problems of life (Ephesians 4:22-24). We now can become trained for the purpose of godliness (1 Timothy 4:7). We now can deny ungodliness and worldly desires and live soberly, righteously and godly (Thus 2:8,9). We can now by the power of the indwelling Holy Spirit, put to death the deeds of the body (which includes sinful anger) and live in a godly and righteous manner (Romans 8:1-13).

What do all these wonderful truths have to do with overcoming sinful anger? Simple answer: Everything! More expansive answer: if people who are Christians continue to be overcome by sinful anger rather than overcoming sinful anger, they do so because they're not choosing to use the resources that God has provided for becoming a godly person (Romans 6:12-22). Developing and expressing sinful anger is not something that has to continue to occur. You can choose to follow the biblical procedure I have outlined in this chapter and learn new ways of handling the challenges of life. The choice is up to you. If this doesn't happen, it's not God's fault, nor is it someone else's fault, nor is it the fault of your circumstances. Ultimately, God's Word would say: it's your fault. You must choose to obey God rather than your own desires. You must choose to trust God rather than yourself. You must choose to practice responding the right way until you are trained in righteousness (I Timothy 4:7; Ephesians 4:22-24; 2 Timothy 3:16).

Many Christians are like the orange juice that may be sitting in our refrigerator. My wife or I may squeeze the juice out of the oranges in the evening, add a little water to it and then put it in the refrigerator to be used in the morning. During the night, however, the good stuff settles to the bottom. So, if we pour out some orange juice without shaking it up or stirring it first, all we get is orange water.

That orange juice is an illustration of what happens with many Christians: They have some basic knowledge of Scripture in their minds, and yet they seem to live as though they didn't know the truths of God's Word at all. When a conflict arises or an unpleasant circumstance occurs, they respond in ways that are contrary to the things they claim they know and believe about godly living. The good stuff is in them, but it's all settled to the bottom; it's not what is gripping and holding and influencing their minds and lives. So they respond to difficulties in the same way unbelievers do with sinful, destructive expressions of anger.

To overcome this tendency Christians need to be constantly stirring up the good stuff – the Word of God – that is in their minds, so that when the difficult times come, they're prepared to respond in a godly way. How do we go about stirring up the good stuff? Part of what we need to do is regularly read, study and memorize God's Word. Part of the stirring process will also involve regularly listening to good, expository, practical teaching of the Bible. However, though doing these things is necessary and excellent, it's only a start. To really be good and angry we need to do even more; we also must apply the things that we have learned to our lives day by day. "But one who looks intently at the perfect law, the law of liberty, and abides by it, not having become a forgetful hearer *but an effectual doer, this man will be blessed in what he does*" (James1:25). In fact, if we fail to do this, God says, "Therefore, to one *who knows the right thing to do and does not do it,* to him it is sin" (James 4:17). As we learn God's commands more and more, we are responsible to obey more and more as well.

One very helpful way of making sure that we actually apply and rightly use God's Word in the existential situations of life, is to commit ourselves to using the questions we've just mentioned to analyze and direct our emotions and behavior in circumstances that may facilitate the development and expression of sinful anger. We need to have a plan and be committed to following that plan at strategic moments in our lives. Most people lose their battles with anger because they go into those battles unprepared.

Let's learn how to overcome sinful anger from the example of Joseph in the book of Genesis. Joseph knew ahead of time that a horrible famine was going to occur in seven years. So what did he do? Did he wait until the famine occurred to decide what to do? No, he knew it was coming and for seven years he got ready. Long before the problem arose he made a plan and then committed himself to following that plan. As a result, he and others were not overcome by the unpleasant event.

That's what we need to do in our battle with anger. As long as we live in this world, we know that unpleasant events are going to occur; we know we're going to face many difficulties. Many stressful situations in which we could become sinfully angry are going to come into our lives. Count on it; this will happen again and again. We can be absolutely certain that just as surely as the famine came to Egypt, we will face circumstances that will tempt us to become sinfully angry. Moreover, we can also be certain that if we, like Joseph, have a plan, and use that plan for handling those occurrences, we can learn to respond to them in a godly, constructive way.

Romans 12:17 says to "Respect what is right in the sight of all men." The Greek word translated "respect" really means that we should plan ahead to do what is right. We cannot just expect to do right; we must *make a plan* to do what is right. We need to think through as many different situations as we can ahead of time and plan our response. "If my spouse does such and such, and I start to become angry, this is what I am going to do. If my children do such and such and I'm tempted to become angry, this is what I'm going to do"

To be good and angry we must make plans and then *practice the plan*. When we get up in the morning, we need to start the day by asking God for help. "Lord, I need your help today. I want to change in this area of my life and be more like Jesus Christ. I now have a plan and today with your help, I want to put my plan into action." Then as we go through our day, we should take time to stop and evaluate our progress.

How did the morning go? "I did fine with my spouse this morning, but I failed when my boss made that comment in our morning meeting." When you've identified your failure, ask God for forgiveness (1 John 1:9). Then you should review and answer the six questions we've previously mentioned and commit yourself to handling the challenges of the afternoon in a more biblical way. In the evening, stop and review again. Ask for God's forgiveness for failures, review and answer the six questions for every failure and recommit yourself to a biblical approach. Follow the same process during the next day and the next and the next. Review, evaluate, and ask for help and forgiveness.

Follow this pattern of putting the plan into practice day after day, until the new pattern becomes a new habit of response. In so doing, you will be training yourself for the purpose of godliness and righteousness (I Timothy 4:7; 2 Timothy 3:16). You will be putting off your old manner of life, which is corrupt and putting on the new manner of life that is righteous and holy (Ephesians 4:22-24).

It will take time to develop this new habit, of course, perhaps much time; probably anywhere from eight to twenty-four weeks of consistent practice. Our bad, unbiblical habits are often slowly changed and exchanged for righteous patterns of living as we renew our minds in God's Word, and put God's Word into practice in our lives. You and I don't have to be angry, hostile people. God's Word says we can change, but it also tells us that change will only occur as we exercise ourselves for the purpose of godliness (I Timothy 4:7; Philippians 2:12).

Some time ago, a man came to me seeking counseling. When I asked him why he had come, he responded, "I have lost my temper and physically abused my wife on many occasions." His anger problem was so serious that the last time it happened, the neighbors called the police. When the police came, he attacked them and was then sent to jail. While in jail, he began to do some serious thinking about his life, his relationship with his wife and other people, and even his relationship with God. A Christian friend (who had witnessed to him before) came to visit him and shared the gospel with him again. By God's grace, this time he heard and was convicted of his sin by the Holy Spirit and began to want to be forgiven and to change his manner of life.

When he was released from jail, his Christian friend encouraged him to seek biblical counseling. He called our counseling center and made an appointment to meet with me. When he first came for counseling, he was separated from his wife. In fact, initially, there was a restraining order against him, preventing him from seeing his wife at all. As we worked together, God began to change this man through the knowledge and power of His Word. He freely acknowledged and repented of his sin, and turned to Christ to receive forgiveness.

He committed himself to the Lordship of Christ and began to develop a love for God's Word, a love for prayer, and a willingness to obey Christ in his life. He became a new creation in Christ, and many of the old things began to pass away and were replaced with the new things of the Christian life. During the time I counseled the man, we taught him the same basic truths about anger that are found in these chapters.

This man embraced these truths and began to faithfully practice the procedure I've described in this chapter.

After several weeks of counseling, the restraining order was lifted and he was allowed to see his wife again. Then, some time after this happened, his wife began to come with him for counseling. It was then my privilege to counsel them together over a period of several months. As we counseled, his way of handling pressures began to change dramatically with other people, but especially with his wife. Instead of responding to his wife with sinful anger, he began to communicate with her in a godly, respectful way. They began to talk through their problems. At that time, they were faced with many trying circumstances such as changing his job, selling their home, getting a new mortgage, and facing the embarrassment of the police incident being reported in the local paper. All of these things put enormous pressure on them as individuals and on their marriage.

God brought these things into this man's life and marriage to test him; to see if he was really serious about his new faith (James 1:2-4; I Peter 1:6-7). It was a joy for me to see how the Lord worked in this man's life through His Word. We used the several questions that I gave earlier in this chapter to help him respond to the pressures of life in a godly way. Though years of sinful habits were difficult to replace with new patterns, this man was able to put these questions to use in his life. Regularly, as he faced potential occasions to which he would have previously responded in sinful ways, he practiced asking himself the questions: *What is happening? What are my thoughts about this situation? What am I not getting that I would like to get and what am I getting that I don't want? What am I tempted to do? What would be the biblical and God-honoring response in this situation? What will I choose to do at this time? Will I obey God or self? Will I do God's will and please Him or will I do my will and please myself?*

I asked him to keep a journal in which he could record the answers to those questions on a daily basis. He did that faithfully, and when he came in for his weekly counseling session, we reviewed that journal. We did that week after week. He noted what he did that he shouldn't have done and what he should have done differently. He would confess his sin and then commit himself to handling situations God's way. Slowly, but surely, as he exercised himself for the purpose of godliness he began to learn a new pattern of response to difficult circumstances.

By God's grace, this man's wife was changed also. Bitterness and resentment had been a pattern throughout her life. From childhood, her mother had rejected her and repeatedly said to her, "God gave you to us to punish us. I wish you had never been born. You are the bane of our existence." This woman initially responded to her mother's cruelty by trying to prove that she was not the bane of her mother's existence. As a child she was very obedient and compliant. Over time, however, she came to realize that she could never win her mother's approval and so she became angry and bitter and quit trying.

This anger toward her mother became very deeply engrained in her life. She told me that there were times when she wished that her mother was dead. At night, she would lie in her bed and picture her mother in a coffin. As you can well imagine, she was a very unhappy, miserable woman. Then she got married and was also mistreated by her husband. In God's goodness, He brought a Christian friend into her life that cared for her and pointed her to Christ through her example and verbal testimony. Through this friend's testimony, she was born again and turned to Christ to receive God's forgiveness; but she needed help in putting off old patterns of thinking and living, and putting on new patterns of thinking and living.

In counseling her, I used the same basic approach that we were using with her husband. I taught her the same basic truths about anger that are found in the chapters in this book. She also embraced these truths and began to practice the same procedure that her husband was employing.

As she exercised herself for the purpose of godliness, we began to see the same changes in her that were taking place in her husband. Their personal lives were being changed. They were becoming more conformed to the image of Christ. They were developing more self-control. They were learning to "walk by the spirit and not fulfill the lusts of the flesh" (Galatians 5:16). They were learning to use God's Word to handle their anger and to experience the power of God in their lives.

Scripture indicates that this kind of power is available to all who are true believers (2 Corinthians 9:8; 1 Corinthians 10:13; Philippians 3:8-11; 2 Corinthians 12:9-10). When we walk by the Spirit and consistently put God's Word into practice, God will help us to change sinful habits. Through the power of the Holy Spirit who lives in us, deeply ingrained sinful patterns of handling the pressures of life can be replaced with godly patterns of response. We can train ourselves for the purpose of godliness. We can learn how to become people whose lives are filled with the fruit of the Spirit rather than the deeds of the flesh. We can put off sinful, destructive, God-displeasing anger and put on righteous, God-honoring and constructive ways of responding to the pressures of life. This chapter gives you a procedure for doing it. Now, the question is, what will you do with the information you have been given?[1]

APPLICATION QUESTIONS

» What is the fourth aspect of learning to be good and angry presented in this chapter?

» What is meant by the statement about harnessing the energy created by our anger?

» What two wrong ways of handling our anger are discussed in this section?

» What are the consequences of handling our anger in either of these two ways?

» What are the six questions that can help us to restrain and replace our sinful anger?

» What important truth does the orange juice illustration teach us about restraining and replacing our sinful anger with a godly response?

» Choose one or two verses that deal with overcoming sinful anger mentioned in this section and write them out in the following space:

_____

_____

_____

_____

» Reflect over the material presented in this chapter and write out the principles (ideas, concepts) that you thought were the most important, helpful, encouraging, convicting ones.

» How will you use this material in your own life or in your ministry to others?

_____

_____

_____

_____

1   The six questions that I have used to help overcome sinful anger
     have been adapted and expanded with my own personal twists from
     materials presented by Dr. Jay Adams and Dr. David Powlison.

CHAPTER 5

WHERE DOES STRESS COME FROM?

Many years ago during what is called the great depression, the most crowd-pleasing gorilla in a certain zoo died. Well, since this happened during the time of the Great Depression, the money to purchase another animal was scarce. So, the zoo managers decided to skin the dead gorilla and hire a man who would get in the skin and act like a gorilla. The man who was hired took his job seriously and since he was very athletic, he developed many crowd-pleasing behaviors. He would grab hold of a bar that would allow him to swing back and forth while doing some spectacular movements. Never before had people seen a gorilla that could do moves that rivaled the moves of an accomplished gymnast or trapeze artist.

One of his most awe inspiring performances involved swinging out over the lion's cage located right next to the gorilla cage. He would swing over that cage, let go with one hand and twirl in various directions while the lion below roared and tried to jump high enough to sink his teeth into his flesh. It was quite a show, and the crowd loved it. One day, however, while swinging out over the lion's cage and doing his most awe-inspiring performances, he lost his grip on the bar and fell into the lion's cage. As the lion roared and came toward him, the man began to yell, "Help! Help! Somebody get me out of here." To the surprise of everyone, especially the man in the gorilla skin, a voice came from the lion saying, "Shut up you fool or we'll both lose our jobs."

At the point when the man inside that gorilla's skin fell into the lion's cage, he found himself in what we could call a very stressful situation. While we may never find ourselves in exactly the same situation, as long as we're in this world we are going to frequently face a variety of stressors. Some of the stressors may seem very minor, and some may seem as serious and dangerous as the man in our story supposed his situation to be. But whether extremely serious or relatively minor, all of us will encounter stressors throughout our entire lives.

Regardless of age, education, social condition, gender or economic status, everyone encounters stressful situations. They simply cannot be avoided. Jesus said, "In the world you will have tribulation ..." (John 16:33). The Psalmist wrote that even though we live a long life, the best of our years will be filled with struggle and turmoil (Psalm 90:10). Job 5:7 reminds us that it's just as certain that we will encounter troubles in our lives as it's that the sparks of a fire will fly upward.

Infants cry in distress. They get hungry, wet, tired or lonely. Children may find going to school, doing their schoolwork, playing sports, or doing their chores stressful. Young people may find dating, trying out for the cheerleading squad, an athletic team, the band or choral group, asking someone out on a date, being rejected as a friend, selecting a college, taking their SAT exams; or choosing a mate a stressful experience. So on through every age of life, people face one challenge after another. The kinds of stressors may vary from person to person and from age to age, but the experience itself does not.

No one can choose whether or not he will face stressors in his life. The only choice we have is how we will be affected by, and respond to, those stressors. The real issue is: How can we overcome the stressors of life before they overcome us? Helping us to know how to overcome rather than be overcome is the purpose of this section of this book. To accomplish this, I will be presenting some key factors in winning, rather than losing, this war against stress.

THE SOURCES OF OUR STRESSORS

To overcome the stressors of life before they overcome us, it's helpful for us to identify the sources of stressors we encounter. We will, in the words of James 1:2, encounter various kinds of trials (stressors).

Some of the stressors may come from our environment or circumstances in our lives. It rains when we're planning to do something that could only be done if it weren't raining. The weather is too hot or too cold for us to be comfortable. We may live in an area where there are earthquakes or where there are severe snowstorms, mudslides or brush fires that threaten to consume our homes. We may be scheduled to be at a certain place at a particular time to speak. We're going by airplane, but the plane arrives late or has mechanical problems that cause the airline to cancel our flight. As a result, we don't make it to the speaking engagement on time, which becomes a stressor for us and also for the people who have asked us to speak. Or we have an appointment to be someplace at 1:00 pm. We leave in plenty of time, but have a flat tire on the way. We try to change the tire as quickly as we can, but the lug nuts simply won't come loose. So we have to call AAA for help that, of course, takes time and makes us late for the appointment.

Unpleasant events we experience, such as things not going as well at work as we would like, a roof that begins to leak, a furnace that breaks down, a job loss, not getting the raise we were counting on, being involved in an automobile accident, or being involved in a business that fails, are all examples of stressors that come into our lives. These stressors often involve things over which we have no direct control. The stressors that come to you from your environment may not be exactly the same as the ones I've just described, but I'm sure you get the picture. You know what I'm talking about and you know how these things can put stress on you.

OUR LIMITATIONS AND DEFICIENCIES

Some of the stressors in our lives come from our own limitations and inadequacies. You look around and see others who are more gifted than you. They have abilities that make it possible for them to do what you would like to be able to do, but can't. Others seem to be doing a better job at what you are trying to do; they seem to be able to work longer, harder and with more success than you do. Consequently, you find yourself asking, "What's wrong with me? Why can't I be as successful or productive as they are?" You can't remember names or facts or procedures and find yourself being embarrassed by your lack of memory.

You see all the work you have to do and wonder how in the world you're going to be able to get it done in a timely fashion. You read Scripture and can't seem to make sense out of it, but then someone else comes along and sees things in the passage that you never imagined were there. You know you ought to be a witness for Christ, but when you're with people you don't know what to say or how to go about it. You want to be a good family leader and influence your family for Christ, but when it comes to leading in devotions or being a good family manager, you judge yourself to be extremely inept.

You compare yourself to what others around you are doing and you find yourself weighed in the balances and coming up short. Why, you even compare yourself to what you used to be able to do, and are disappointed in what you find happening. You come to the conclusion that you're going in the wrong direction and losing ground in terms of your own personal progress.

A number of years ago, my wife and I had our fourth child when we were thirty-nine years of age. Joshua was born eight years after our third child. We discovered that eight years had made a difference in what we could physically do. At thirty-nine, my wife wasn't what you would call old, but child birth at thirty nine took more out of her than the previous ones. People would ask us, "Is it more difficult for you to get down and play with Joshua than it was with your other children?" We responded, "No, it's not more difficult to get down, but it surely is a lot more difficult to get up!" The point I'm making with all of this is that the aging process and the implications thereof can be sources of stress even if you don't have a child at thirty-nine.

An interaction I had while counseling a depressed sixty year-old woman illustrates how the changes that occur as people become older can be a stressor.

This woman complained that she was experiencing depression because she wasn't able to accomplish as much as she previously had been able to accomplish. I asked her, "What are you not able to do that you previously had been able to do?" She answered, "Oh, many things. I just don't seem to be able to get anything done."

Since her answer was so general, I gave her a homework assignment that would give me some specific information about what was really going on in her life. I had her keep a daily journal of what she did

during the day. At the next session when I perused the journal she gave
to me, I noticed that she was very active and, from my perspective,
seemed to be accomplishing a lot. When I mentioned that to her she
responded, "Yes, but I used to be able to do a lot more." I said to her,
"As you grow older, you can't expect to have the same energy and
physical strength that you had when you were younger." I surmised by
watching her facial expression as I spoke those words to her that she
didn't like what I had said. I was right, because I had no sooner finished
speaking when she retorted, "I'm not old, and I don't want to grow old."
I allowed her to finish her statement and then I gently responded, "You
may not want to grow old, but whether you like it or not, you are going
to grow old. You'd better learn to accept that fact and rejoice in the
benefits of older age rather than fighting it. If you don't, you're going
to be miserable for the rest of your life. And besides that, why does it
bother you to be getting older? What is it that makes you dislike getting
older so much?"

This woman was being overcome by the stress of her own perceived
limitations. She is not alone in this regard. In one way or another,
every one of us will experience stressors that come to us from our own
limitations and deficiencies as we go through life; deficiencies that may
be intellectual, physical, social, financial, relational, or spiritual. At
every age, our own limitations and deficiencies can become a stressor
in our lives.

OTHER PEOPLE

By far, the most common stressors we face in life have something to
do with other people. There's a story about two porcupines that were
living close to one another in Alaska. One winter when the weather was
especially cold they got the idea that maybe if they huddled together
they could keep each other warm. They agreed and so they tried it, but
soon decided it wasn't such a good idea after all. They discovered that
as they tried to huddle together they were needling each other rather
than warming each other.

That story illustrates what often happens in our relationships with
people. It seems that the closer we get to people, the more we get
needled. What often happens is summed up in the little quip that says,
"Oh, to dwell there above with the saints that we love, that will be glory.
But to dwell here below with the saints that we know, that's another
story." When a certain person came home from church one Sunday

morning he said to his mother, "Mother I'm never going back to that church again." His mother replied, "Son, tell me who you're never going back to that church again." "I'm never going back to that church again because it's impossible to get along with those people. They don't listen to me. They don't care about me. They just aren't very nice." "Well son," the mother responded, "you are going back to that church and I'll give you two reasons why. First, you're going back because you're forty years-old and second, you're going back because you're the pastor."

The aforementioned pastor was learning that getting along with people could be a real challenge. The truth is that our relationships with people can be a great source of joy, and they can also be a great source of heartache.

As we go through life, we can count on the fact that we will experience stressors in our lives, and we can also be sure that many of those stressors will have something to do with people. Obviously, God knows this and that is why there is so much in the Bible about the importance and difficulty of maintaining good relationships with people.

Good relationships don't just automatically happen; they require a lot of work to achieve and sustain. John Trapp, the Puritan preacher and commentator was right when he said, "It is unlikely that you could put two sinners together and not have some conflicts, as it's that you could strike two pieces of flint together and not have some sparks." According to Jesus, peace with people is not something that happens automatically: it's something we must endeavor to make (Matthew 5:8). According to the apostle Paul, we must be diligent and put forth a lot of effort if we're going to preserve unity with people (Ephesians 4:3). In James 1:2, we are reminded that in life we're going to face many different kinds of trials (stressors). The rest of the book of James makes it clear that the source of many of these trials will involve getting along with other people.

Understanding that we will face stressors as we travel life's journey and knowing what the sources of these stressors will most likely be can be very helpful in properly handling those trials when they do come.

TYPICAL RESPONSES TO THE STRESSORS OF LIFE

Identifying the wrong ways we are prone to respond to the stressors we encounter in life can help us to avoid the wrong, ungodly and destructive responses to them. The old saying that "to be forewarned is to be forearmed" has a ring of truth in it. Being forewarned isn't all that's necessary to get the job done, but it can be useful. Knowing how we are prone to respond may help us to be alert and on guard against these wrong responses. Jesus indicates that being on the alert and watching is an important part of resisting temptation (Matthew 26:41).

DEBILITATING FEAR OR ANXIETY

One of these wrong responses that we must be on guard against is debilitating fear. One person I know is extremely afraid of storms. She lives in constant fear of thunder and lightning. When a storm comes she is paralyzed by it, and when it's not storming, she lives in fear that a storm might come. Having lived in California, I know that there are people who live in constant fear that there might be another earthquake, or that California may drop off into the ocean. I know people who will not visit California because they're afraid that while they're there an earthquake might occur, or others who have moved out of California because of their fear of earthquakes.

Having also lived in Pennsylvania, which can be quite cold and snowy in the wintertime, I've met people who are constantly complaining about how horrible it is to live in such a place. They dread the cold and snow, and are constantly talking about how nice it would be to live elsewhere. For some people, being in a crowd is a frightening thing, and so their lives are inhibited by the fear of being in crowds of people. Some people live in constant fear that they might lose their job, get sick, or that something horrible will happen to them or their family. For some, they fear that an endeavor in which they're involved may fail, or that they might be rejected or make fools out of themselves. Fear of people causes some to withdraw from people or activities; it causes them to be nervous when in the presence of people who are physically beautiful or people who have a high position, a lot of money or intelligence and knowledge.

Fear can take many forms (I've only mentioned a few), but regardless of what form it takes, it's inhibiting. Inordinate, debilitating fear is a wrong response to the stressors of life. Scripture, of course, is right on target when it tells us that fear brings a snare and that it brings punishment and torment (Proverbs 29:25; I John 4:18). According to Scripture, fear that keeps us from living the kind of life that God wants us to live is unnecessary and extremely destructive. In numerous places, God commands us not to fear and tells us why there are no justifiable reasons for this debilitating fear response to the stressors of life (e.g., Isaiah 41:10; I John 4:18-19; Proverbs 28:10).

WORRY OR ANXIETY

Closely connected to the response of debilitating fear is the response of anxiety, or what is more commonly called worry. Worry usually focuses on what may happen if something does or doesn't occur (cf. Matthew 6:34). However, it's not limited to an inordinate concern about the future; it can also be a response to what has happened or is happening. A person worries when thoughts about the past, present or future consume and constrain that person in some way.

Worry is usually associated with something that appears threatening, something that you perceive may harm your safety; something that you would like to control, but are overly concerned that you can't control. You don't worry about something that you don't consider a threat to any of the things I've just mentioned. Worry always carries with it the idea that you, or someone you care about, may be harmed by whatever it is you are worrying about. There is such a thing as eustress (good stress) that is productive and positive; worry bleeds over into distress (bad stress) that is counter productive and negative.

Unfortunately, the lives of some people can be summarized in the three words, "hurry, worry and bury." All too often the lifestyle of many people is a lifestyle in which anxiety has become their habitual way of responding to the stressors of life. This, of course, is a wrong response to stressors in that the Bible not only frequently tells us not to worry, but also encourages us with the good news that we can experience a peace that passes understanding (cf., Matthew 6:25-34; Philippians 4:6- 7; John 14:1- 27).

BITTERNESS, ANGER AND RESENTMENT

Bitterness, anger and resentment when encountering the stressors of life is another common, but ungodly way, of handling the various situations we face in life. In my counseling ministry I have frequently seen this response played out in marriage relationships. This, for example, is the way many women respond to their husbands when their mates won't communicate with them in the way they desire, or won't do something they want them to do. Likewise, this is the way some men habitually respond to their wives or children, or anyone else when they're not pleased with the treatment they're getting. With these men or women, it's "You do it my way when I want you to do, and how

I want you to do it, or you're in trouble!"

The Bible contains examples of many people who responded to the stressors that they encountered in this way. The book of I Samuel describes how Saul responded in a similar way to his son Jonathan, and his friend, David. Genesis 4 tells us that Cain responded this way to God and to his brother Abel. Genesis 27 gives us an illustration of this kind of response in the case of Esau with his brother Jacob. Even the great prophet Jonah handled the pressure of unfulfilled desires and unwanted circumstances by becoming angry (Jonah 4).

Many passages of Scripture speak clearly about the error of this response. Here is a sampling: "Let all (not some, but all) bitterness and wrath and anger…. be put away from you with all malice" (Ephesians 4:31). "Let your forbearing spirit be known to all (not some, but all) men" (Philippians 4:5). "But now you also, put them all (not some, but all) aside: anger, resentment, malice…" (Colossians 3:8).

DEPRESSION AND DISCOURAGEMENT

As noted previously, the man Cain not only illustrates that anger is a very common response to stressors; but, in addition to that, he also illustrates that depression, gloom or discontentment are common responses to stressors. Scripture says he became angry and his countenance fell ("he became very depressed"--Berkely version). His disappointment, depression and dissatisfaction over not getting his own way was so great that it manifested itself on his face or in his demeanor (cf. Genesis 4).

I Kings 21 indicates that when circumstances didn't work out the way Ahab desired, he was very vexed. In fact, he was so upset, so disappointed because of what did and didn't happen, that he went home, went up to his bedroom, crawled into his bed, turned his face to the wall and refused to eat. Never mind that he had kingly responsibilities, or that he was being childish and petulant. At this point, though to an extreme, Ahab typifies a very common response to the stressors of life.

In contrast to this way of handling the stressors of life the Bible says: "Rejoice in the Lord always (not just occasionally, but always)" (Phil. 4:4). "Finally, my brethren, rejoice in the Lord" (Philippians 3:1). "Rejoice always" (I Thessalonians 5:16). "Let your life be free from the love of money, being content with what you have…" (Hebrews 13:5). "If we have food and covering, with these we shall be content" (I Tim. 4:8).

ENVY AND JEALOUSY

Going back to the Cain illustration, we note another very typical ungodly response to the stressors we encounter. Cain was angry, despondent, miserable and unhappy; he was also very envious and jealous of his brother. His brother had received something he wanted very badly. Abel had been approved, accepted, recognized and rewarded while Cain had not. Instead of rejoicing at his brother's good fortune or learning from his brother's example, as Proverbs 6:34 states, Cain's jealousy caused him to lash out in vengeance against his brother. Thus, Cain's response to the stressor of seeing his brother honored above himself becomes a vivid illustration of the truth of Proverbs 27:4: "Wrath is fierce and anger is a flood, but who can stand before jealousy?"

In 3 John, Diotrophes functioned in the same way: To see others honored and respected was a stressful situation for him. He couldn't stand it when the early Christians showed respect to the apostle John and other early church leaders. Because of his jealousy, he refused to accept anything they said and openly attacked them, making wicked and slanderous accusations. What's more, he exercised unreasonable authority in forbidding others to have anything to do with John and other church leaders.

The first chapter of Philippians refers to men in the early church who were jealous of the respect Paul received from other Christians. For them, it was extremely stressful to see the concern and appreciation that many in the early church had for Paul and his ministry. Their jealousy was so strong that they actually tried to make things worse for Paul, who already was in prison for his commitment to Christ. Somehow they thought, by making things worse for Paul, things would be better for them.

I wonder what is going through your mind as you read these jealous responses the people gave to the stressors. You might say, "How could they be that selfish and ungodly?" Do you say, "Thank you Lord that I'm not like these people"? Or, do you recognize that you have at times reacted to, or have been tempted to react to, the successes of others in a somewhat similar way?

Honesty would compel many of us to admit that we have not done enough rejoicing with those who rejoice (Romans 12:15); that we have not always been devoted to others in brotherly love and preferred to honor others above ourselves (Romans 12:10). Who of us can say that we have done nothing out of selfishness and vain conceit, and that in humility of mind we have always esteemed others as more important than ourselves (Philippians 2:3)?

ANNOYANCE, IRRITABILITY AND IMPATIENCE

The ungodly response of choice for many of us in pressure situations is irritability, annoyance or impatience, which is expressed on our faces, words and actions. When under pressure, we may be brusque, curt, insensitive and inconsiderate of the feelings of other people. When under pressure, we may have a tendency to respond in the way Martha did as described in Luke 10:38-42: By being pushy, demanding, brusque, somewhat rude and unjustly accusatory. This was the way the elder brother handled the stressor he was experiencing at the return of his younger brother. On this occasion, he lashed out at his father and made some very unkind and untrue remarks. At this point, he had no regard for how his words and actions would impact his father or brother. He was irritated and he just let loose and lambasted his father.

I must admit that on occasion I'm tempted to respond to stressors in an impatient manner. I've analyzed when and with whom this is most likely to occur. From my analysis, I've discerned that I'm most likely to become impatient when demands are made on me that I think are unrealistic, or when I have too much to do. At that point I wonder how I'm going to get it all done when others have expectations of me that I simply can't fulfill, or when others interrupt me while I'm doing something I think is important and needs to get done, misrepresent what I have done or said, or ask questions to which the answers are obvious. Experience has taught me that I'm not tempted to respond this way with everyone, but only with certain people. In particular, I have identified who those people are, and even the kind of people with whom I have the most trouble being patient.

For me, understanding the dynamics of my impatience has been helpful in the sanctification process of developing more godly responses to the stressors in my life. Being forewarned of the possibility of this happening has encouraged me to be forearmed against it happening. Being aware of the identity of the people with whom I may react this way helps me to prevent it from occurring. It has also promoted an increased alertness and sensitivity to my sin, which facilitates a more speedy confession to God and anyone who happens to be on the receiving end of my impatience.

DENIAL AND PRETENSE

In studying Scripture and working with people (including myself) for many years, I have noticed that they often practice denial in reference to their response to stressors. That is, they deny the fact that something is bothering them, even if it is. They pretend that everything is okay with them when in reality it's not.

Since God knows that people respond this way, we could expect that this response would be mentioned in Scripture, and it is! For example, in Prov. 26:23-28 we find a description of people who have fervent lips (lips that burn with positive, agreeable, pleasant words to your face) while on the inside these people have an evil heart. Still further, this passage refers to people who speak graciously, but while everything seems to be fine outwardly, inwardly they have seven abominations in their hearts. According to the text, these people cover what is really going on in their hearts with deception; they flatter people with their mouths while hating them in their hearts.

Matthew 23:27 mentions people who outwardly appear righteous, but inwardly they're full of hypocrisy and lawlessness. Luke 11:39 presents the same picture in that it refers to people who are clean on the outside, but full of greed and wickedness on the inside. Psalm 28:3 is talking about the same common phenomenon when it tells us that some people speak outwardly about peace, while evil (hatred, malice, resentment, a desire to hurt and harm) is in their hearts. The admonition of Ephesians 4:25 to put away falsehood and speak the truth with others certainly would include the practice of pretending that everything is all right when it really isn't. Denial to the Lord, yourself or to other people is a form of falsehood; it's a failure to speak the truth. It's an ungodly and unhelpful way of responding to the stressors of life that must be changed.

As mentioned earlier, pouring out wicked words and performing malicious actions when under stress are wrong ways of responding to stressors, but then, so is the practice of denial. Denying that you are disturbed doesn't make the problem go away any more than exploding does. Recognizing and admitting that you are being affected by what's happening, and learning how to appropriately respond to the stressor is the biblical way of overcoming stress before it overcomes you. In a future chapter I will discuss a specific procedure, but for now let us review and seek to apply what has been written in this chapter.

We have noted two important factors in overcoming stress before it overcomes us: First, I have noted that if we want to overcome stress before it overcomes us, we should be aware of the different kinds of stressors we are most apt to experience. Second, I have stated that to overcome stress we should identify the particularly sinful ways in which we are most prone to respond to the stressors we encounter and to be on guard against them. Additionally, by implication, I have also suggested that we should analyze our own lives to determine which of the sinful responses we are most prone to practice. Doing this analysis would involve: 1) identifying when we are most apt to respond in an ungodly manner; 2) discovering with whom it's most likely to occur; and 3) quickly seeking God's forgiveness and the forgiveness of others when we respond in this unbiblical way.

APPLICATION QUESTIONS

» Identify some of the different categories of the most common sources of stress in the lives of people.

» In what ways can (do) our environment become a circumstantial cause of our stress?

» In what ways can (do) our own limitations become a circumstantial cause of our stress?

» In what ways can (do) other people become a circumstantial cause of our stress?

» In what ways can (do) past or future events become a circumstantial cause of our stress?

» Identify which of these common sources of stress are most problematic to you.

» How would the Bible describe the main reasons we get stressed out? What are the various wrong (unbiblical) ways that people respond to stressful circumstances?

» Besides the wrong responses mentioned in this chapter, what other wrong responses to stress have you observed people using?

» To which of these unbiblical ways of responding to potentially stressful circumstances are you most prone?

» What were the most important challenging and convicting truths that you received from this chapter?

CHAPTER 6

THERE ARE CONSEQUENCES

In the previous chapter on overcoming stress, I used the well-known phrase, "To be forewarned is to be forearmed." That's a good statement; but, perhaps, we should alter it to say, "To be forewarned is part of the process of becoming forearmed." Warnings, if they're accurate, are helpful, but they're not enough. They're necessary, but they don't automatically arm us. What they can do is provide the motivation for us to want to be armed for battle. Hopefully, that's what the last chapter, and the material found in this chapter, will do for you and me.

In the previous chapter on overcoming stress, I stated that:

1. It's helpful to identify the different sources of the stressors we face; answering the question, "Where do they come from?" can help us to be forewarned.

2. It's beneficial to identify the common wrong responses to stressors in general, but in particular, it's even more useful to identify the kinds of ungodly responses to which we personally are most prone.

In chapters seven and eight of this book, I want to describe a more specific plan of operation for winning the war against the stressors that would destroy us; but before I do that, I want to continue the forewarning process by describing for you a few of the serious consequences that are produced by our ungodly responses to stressors. I do this because this is one of the methods God uses in His Word to keep us from making bad choices and to motivate us to think before we act.

By including many statements in His Word about the consequences of certain actions and many examples of people who made bad choices and suffered serious, unpleasant consequences, God is trying to do two things. First, He is trying to prevent us from making the same mistakes over and over again. Second, He is trying to motivate us to make wise choices. My hope is that a discussion of the serious consequences of our wrong responses to stress will function in these two ways for us. Here then are a few of the serious consequences of the wrong responses to stress.

CONSEQUENCE #1: POOR RELATIONSHIPS WITH PEOPLE

On the other hand, You show me a person whose life is characterized by the fruit of the Spirit as he faces the stressors of life, and I will show you a person who is well respected by people; a person who has a good marriage; a good family; and a person who has many good friends. On the other hand, you show me a person who responds to stress by not doing what Ephesians 4:31 tells us, and I'll show you a person who has problems in his relationships with people.

For almost forty years, I've been involved in counseling people with problems. During that time I've heard many people who have told me they have no friends. One fifty-five year-old man told me that he has never had a close friend in his whole life. Being in a position where I could observe the way he relates to his wife and children and to other people in the church, I have seen him acting and reacting in many of the ways described in the last chapter. Around people he tightens up, withdraws, pulls into himself, runs away rather than reaching out to people, and waits for them to come to him rather than him going to them. Gloom and doom are written all over his face. He expects the worst and usually, because of his attitude, gets it.

The consequences: he has only superficial relationships with people; he misses out on the benefits that God has planned to bring into our lives through deep relationships with people; he fails to fulfill the ministries that God wants him to have through deep relationships with people; and he experiences the pain of loneliness.

CONSEQUENCE # 2: STULTIFICATION OF SPIRITUAL GROWTH

What happens when you go to church after you've had a big conflict with your mate or children, and then tried to get something out of the Sunday School lesson or sermon? You don't really benefit from that act of worship, do you? At least, I find it difficult to do so, and I know of others who have had the same experience. Or, what happens when you try to read or study your Bible or pray after you've blown it by being selfish and nasty? Well, if your conscience is functioning properly and if you have not repented, confessed, and sought forgiveness, your spiritual appetite, sensitivity and receptivity to spiritual things will be affected. Stultification of our spiritual growth is the inevitable result.

In light of what God has said in many passages of Scripture, it can't be otherwise. Mark 4 asserts that the cares and anxieties of this world choke the Word and make it unfruitful. I Peter 3:7 states that if a man is not living with his wife in an understanding, caring and respectful way, his devotional life will be hindered. In similar fashion, James 1:20-25 indicates that if we don't deal with the sin patterns in our lives, we will not receive the blessing that God intends for us to have through His Word. If we don't deal with our sin, God won't hear us—and guess what?— we won't hear from God through His Word either. "He that confesses and forsakes his sin shall have mercy" is God's Word to us (Proverbs 28:13).

Does this make wrong responses to the stressors of life a serious matter? You'd better believe it does! Could it be that many of us are standing still or, worse yet, going backwards in our spiritual lives because we are being overcome by rather than overcoming stress? We may excuse our sinful responses and take them lightly, but God doesn't.

CONSEQUENCE # 3: LACK OF SPIRITUAL USEFULNESS

Right along with the fact that our ungodly responses hinder our spiritual growth is the fact that they hinder our spiritual usefulness. A clear passage on this matter is 2 Timothy 2:21, which tells us that "If a man cleanses himself, he will be a vessel for honor, sanctified, useful to the Master, prepared for every good work." This verse teaches that if a person doesn't cleanse him or herself from what God calls wickedness and ungodliness (cf. 2:16-19), he will not be a vessel that will honor God and be honored by God in his ministry for Christ. If he doesn't cleanse himself, he won't be useful to the Master and prepared for every good work. In Luke 8:14, our Lord Jesus Christ said essentially the same thing: A person who responds in an ungodly way to the pressures and temptations of life will bring no fruit to maturity.

People who typically and frequently respond to the stressors of life in any of the ungodly ways described in the previous chapter are like the fig tree described in Matthew 21. This tree had had leaves but bore no fruit. They're like the farmer who sows a lot of seeds, but none of it ever seems to germinate. They're in the words of Jude 12, "clouds without water," "autumn trees without fruit."

What I'm referring to are people who may be very active in some form of Christian service, and yet their service doesn't seem to be bearing much fruit; people who may be busy in Christian ministries, but little is being accomplished through them by way of evangelism of unbelievers or edification of believers. I'm speaking of people of whom it can't be said that they're really building up the body of Christ (Ephesians 4:12-16). Oh, these people may have great gifts, they may have a lot of knowledge, they may be very biblically correct in their theology; but in a very real sense they aren't making an impact for Christ in helping others to become like Him. Sometimes this is true because they haven't cleansed themselves from their ungodly responses to the stressors of life.

Paul's words to Timothy in I Timothy 4:12 are very appropriate at this point. In effect he said, "Timothy, if you want people to respect you and your message, you'd better be a model of that message in your love (for Christ and people), purity (in heart, mind and conduct), faith (trust and confidence in Christ and His Word), faithfulness (trustworthiness, reliability, dependability), speech (content, manner, purpose). In other words, if you want to have a fruitful ministry, you'd better be a model of the power of the Gospel making you different on the inside and outside, in your actions and reactions. *If you don't handle stress differently than unbelievers, don't expect to make an impact for Christ.*

Habitually responding improperly to the stressors of life will also affect a person's Christian service activities in another way: Sometimes it will weaken or even destroy his desire and confidence in even attempting to serve. This is illustrated by a conversation I had with a professing Christian man. This man (we'll call him "Jim") told me that he didn't witness for Christ at work because he knew his life wasn't what it ought to be. (Actually, he did witness. Unfortunately, as you will see from my report, the witness he was giving by his life was against Christ, rather than for Christ.) But let's get back to the actual conversation. Jim said, "I don't witness for Christ at work because I'm ashamed to do so. I know the people with whom I work see my selfishness, my greed, my anxiety, and my angry responses. They hear my griping and complaining. Consequently, I don't think they would be interested in what I say because they don't see me as a good example of what a Christian should be."

I don't know if that was the main reason Jim didn't witness, but I do know that what he said was true, and that his awareness of his own sin stultified his desire to witness for Christ. And, I also know that what was true of Jim is true of many other people as well. Because of their habitual ungodly responses to the stressors of life, they're not prepared for every good work, and besides that, their ungodly actions and reactions have caused their desire to be useful to the Master to be snuffed out.

CONSEQUENCE # 4: HINDERED OCCUPATIONAL AND EDUCATIONAL ACHIEVEMENTS

Many competent people have lost job after job because they have frequently responded in some of the ungodly ways described in the last chapter. Or, if they haven't been dismissed from their jobs, they have not advanced in their jobs because they're so uptight, nervous, easily flustered, annoyed, fearful, or anxious. They just can't handle the pressure; they react excessively to criticism and consequently they're overlooked when it comes to the matter of advancement.

Over the course of my forty or more years in counseling people, I have met many who have a good education and skills that you would think would make them very successful in their occupation. Yet, they go from job to job; they never last long in any place of employment. Sometimes, they just up and quit, and sometimes they're "let go" (i.e., fired). I can think of many missionaries and pastors who have been like the proverbial "rolling stone," only staying in any one place of ministry for a brief period of time. Often, if not usually, the reason is that they're aren't handling the stressors they inevitably experience in a godly way.

In the educational realm, I know of students who have good minds and yet have done very poorly in their schoolwork. With some, it was because they never disciplined themselves to do some hard studying.

With others, though they spent hours on their homework, they just squeaked by on their tests. Why? Outside of class when talking to others in private, they demonstrated they knew the material. When test time came, it was a different matter; they froze, their minds went blank; they experienced test anxiety and drew a mental block.

CONSEQUENCE # 5: PHYSICAL PROBLEMS

Scripture and modern science both agree on the serious consequences that the wrong responses to stress can have on the human body. In Scripture we read that "Anxiety in the heart weighs it down"; "Passion (unrest in the inner man, viz.; anger, depression, discouragement, worry, fear, annoyance, impatience) is rottenness to the bones (i.e., is bad for your health; weakens you); "a broken spirit dries up the bones" (bones that are dried up are easily broken; they're brittle, fragile and therefore they are very unstable and untrustworthy) (Proverbs 12:25; 14:30; 17:22).

As might be expected, modern medical studies illustrate the validity of these biblical statements. In his book, *None of These Diseases*, Dr. S. I. McMillen lists more than sixty diseases that either are caused by or aggravated by wrong responses to stress.[1] One chapter, for example is entitled, "It's not What You Eat; It's What is Eating You."

Several years ago the head of the gastrointestinal surgery department at a major hospital in Philadelphia attended one of my biblical counseling training courses. One evening after class, he told me how much he agreed with what I had been teaching about understanding and solving the problems of people biblically. In the course of our conversation, he said that he believed that at least sixty-five percent of the people he operated on wouldn't need the operations he performed if they'd only learn how to handle their stressors in a biblical way.

Another Christian physician friend informed me that he was convinced that many of the physical problems people have are somehow connected to the way they live their lives and respond to the stresses they encounter. In fact, he was so convinced of this that a few years ago he was tempted to leave the medical field and join the staff of a church where he would do biblical counseling full time. He stated that he considered making this move because he thought he could do more good for people physically and spiritually by helping them to prevent and solve their problems through practical, biblical teaching and counsel.

What happens when people don't handle stressors in life in a godly way? In his book, *The Christian Counselors' Medical Desk Reference*, physician Robert Smith writes:

> Responses to various circumstances in life may themselves produce symptoms of sickness. God created various internal controls to maintain balance in the body. One of the controls is the hormone system. This system functions on the basis of supply and demand. If there is too little hormone in the body, the gland responsible for it produces more. If there is too much hormone, the gland decreases the amount produced. All this happens automatically.

> Another control system is the nervous system (NS), which is made up of the brain, spinal cord, and nerves. Reflexes provide many NS controls. A certain stimulus produces specific results. When you accidentally touch something hot, automatic reflexes make the muscles pull the hand away from the hot object. These controls are essential to balance within the body. A very significant fact is that these controls may be influenced by circumstances in life. Those responses may produce physical symptoms.

> A person's evaluation of, and responses to, various circumstances in life will produce symptoms in the body. Pastors may remember their ordination council as an awesome and fearful time. There is a desire to do a good job, along with considerable apprehension about the kind of questions that may be asked. This response to the anticipation of the council may produce symptoms in the body. His mouth may become dry as he prepares to answer a question. His heart and breathing rate may speed up to deliver more fuel to the cells of the body and remove more waste products. There may be a fine tremor of the muscles. The effect on the intestinal tract may be varied. The stomach may be undecided about whether it's going to empty up or down....The lower bowel may even become very irritable and spastic. The result may be cramping or diarrhea. All these symptoms are the result of one's response to the pressure of the ordination examination.

> The intestinal tract is a tube with muscles in two directions: around the circumference of the tube and down the length of the tube. ...

These muscles can cramp like a 'charley horse', which in turn produces pain. This is one of the ways in which an ulcer in the first part of the small intestine (the duodenum) produces pain. Extra acid produced in the stomach as a result of a person's response to problems will also irritate the exposed ulcerated tissue. (The same cramping happens in irritable bowel disease without the increased acid production.)

Unbiblical responses to life and difficult situations can produce the same cramping as that of an ulcer. …The counselor should be aware that such physical symptoms may be caused by the person's response to life and problems.

The person's response to problems has produced symptoms and may produce disease.

…in sixty to eighty percent of patients, responses to problems of life produced physical symptoms…these symptoms are not imaginary. They're physical. They're real, but they're not triggered by something wrong in the body.

The real problem then is not your counselee's problems, but his response to those problems. A person often cannot change pressures or tough circumstances, but he can change his responses to them.[2]

In summary, I will adapt and modify Dr. Smith's diagram that illustrates the manner in which the physical part of us is affected by our responses to the stressors in our lives.

1. Life's Experiences (which include):

Problems we experience
Pressures we face
Difficulties we encounter
Trials that come our way

2. Our evaluation of these experiences and reaction to them produces effects on the body in the:

Mouth – dry mouth
Heart – rate increases

Lungs – breath more deeply, even hyper ventilate. difficulty breathing
Muscles – tense, tighten, cramp
Intestinal tract – cramps, diarrhea, constipation, colitis

As we've seen, it's easy to see why I say that responding wrongly to the stressors of life is a rather serious matter. Hopefully, by this time all of us are saying, "What must we do to keep from responding in the wrong way to stressors, and from experiencing the destructive consequences that come when we do?" If that's what you're saying, I'm glad because that's what we're going to discuss in the next two chapters.

APPLICATION/DISCUSSION QUESTIONS

» List the destructive consequences of ungodly responses to stress mentioned in this chapter.

» What impact or effect do these wrong responses have? In what ways do they really hinder us?

» Besides the consequences described in this chapter, can you think of any other consequences of these wrong responses?

» Can you give any illustrations of someone (yourself or someone else) experiencing any of the consequences discussed in this chapter?

» How could you use the material in this chapter in your own life, your family's, or with other people?

» In your judgment, what were the most important concepts or insights presented in this chapter?

1   op. cit.
2   *The Christian Counselor's Medical Desk Reference*, pp. 41-46

CHAPTER 7

THE WAY OF ESCAPE – PART 1

From all we've noted thus far, we can see that responding wrongly to the stressors of life is a rather serious matter. In the next two chapters, we'll discuss what we must do to avoid reacting wrongly to the stressors of life. We will begin by laying out some key factors in a biblical procedure for overcoming stress before it overcomes you.

OVERCOMING FACTOR # 1

To win this battle over the stressors of life, you must deliberately choose to see everything that happens to you within the framework of the Sovereignty of God.

Believing and applying the truth of Ephesians 1:11 that God "works all things after the counsel of His will" will inevitably have a positive effect on the way we handle stress. The words "all things" remind us of the scope of God's control. Perhaps we could discuss whether this statement is referring to what some people call God's "permissive will" or His "will of ordination." We can discuss whether God permits or ordains all the events and experiences that enter our lives. Either way, the point is that God is in charge of what happens in the universe and in your life. If you take the position that God permits, but doesn't ordain all things that happen, you still must realize that He, being the loving, wise, gracious, all-powerful God that He is, could have prevented it if He had chosen to do so. Moreover, if He didn't prevent it, you must realize that He has a definite purpose for allowing it to happen. The fact is He works all things in accordance with the counsel of His will. Therefore, if He didn't will it to occur, it wouldn't have occurred.

Throughout the Bible, this great truth about God's sovereignty over everything in general as well as the events of our lives is clearly spelled out. I will quote a few of these many references because this truth is the foundational truth for developing a biblical procedure for overcoming the stressors of life. One text with enormous implications for overcoming stress is found in Matthew 10:29. Here our Lord Jesus Christ teaches that not even a sparrow dies apart from God's will.

The point of this passage is not simply that God knows when a sparrow dies. Rather, Jesus is saying much more than that: He is asserting that a sparrow doesn't die unless it's the will of God that it should expire. By saying this, our Lord Jesus Christ wants us to know, and be comforted by the fact, that if God is involved with the death of something as insignificant as a sparrow, He is certainly involved in, and vitally concerned about, everything that happens to His own children.

The truth of Psalm 103:19, when rightly understood and applied, will be a transforming influence in the life of a believer as he faces pressure. This text tells us that God's throne has been established in the heavens and that He, in His sovereignty, rules over all. Daniel 4:34-35 says much the same thing in a more expansive way: "His dominion is an everlasting dominion, and His Kingdom endures from generation to generation. All the inhabitants of the earth are accounted as nothing (i.e., in comparison to Him), but He does according to His will in the host of heaven and among the inhabitants of earth: No one can ward off His hand or say to Him, "What have you done?" God, according to this text, is so absolutely sovereign and perfect that no one has a right or should even think about putting Him on the witness stand to give an accounting of what He has done.

Psalm 37:23 reminds us that the steps of a person who has been made righteous in God's sight through Christ are ordered by the Lord. Note carefully what this text says. It tells us that God orders this person's "steps," not just the overall plan for his life. If words mean anything, this means that God is deeply involved in the details of this person's life. Note, still further, that the verse says that this person's steps are "ordered." That is, that what happens in a person's life doesn't just happen haphazardly or by chance. It means that there is some order to what happens. Who does the ordering? Being true to the text leads us to only one conclusion: The Lord does the ordering.

Romans 8:28 has long been a favorite of believers as they face the stressors of life. What is the message of this text? It's that God is deeply involved in what happens to a believer. In all and over all of the events of a believer's life, God is working for the believer's good. It's that nothing happens that is outside God's control. It's that God can and does orchestrate and order the events in a Christian's life, so that even that which is painful and unpleasant will be used by God to produce something good. If God weren't sovereign over all things, including the events of our lives, this verse would be sheer gibberish and would make no sense at all. We would have no reason to believe that what it clearly says will come to pass. However, if we really believe what it says and plug its obvious meaning and implications into our thinking during a time of stress, we will find the ungodly responses discussed in chapter five minimized and even eliminated.

The Bible has many illustrations of the practical value of believing and applying the doctrine of God's sovereignty during a time of stress. In terms of the roster of people who experienced severe pressure, Joseph has to be near the top of the list. He was mocked and badly mistreated by other family members. He had come to them on an errand of mercy, but they captured him and threw him into a pit. While he was in that pit, no doubt within earshot, his brothers debated about what they could do to get rid of him. Some of them voted for killing him, but then another brother suggested that they should sell him into slavery and even make some money in the deal. That's precisely what they did.

As a result, Joseph became the indentured slave of a man named Potiphar, whose wife wanted to seduce him into an immoral relationship. When Joseph refused her advances, Mrs. Potiphar became so angry that she went to her husband and accused Joseph of being a rapist. As a result of her lies, Joseph was thrown into prison. How long he was there we don't know. We do know, however, that while he was in prison he helped a man who had been in the service of Pharaoh to understand the meaning of a dream that he had. In his interpretation, Joseph indicated that the man would be released from prison and returned to his responsible position with Pharaoh. In the process of assisting this man, Joseph asked him to intercede with Pharaoh on his behalf after he was released and restored. The man agreed and not long after that, the predictions of Joseph were fulfilled.

When that took place, Joseph had every reason to believe that this servant of the Pharaoh would fulfill his promise and intercede on his behalf. Unfortunately, for what would appear to be a considerable period of time, the man forgot about the arrangement he had made with Joseph (Genesis 40:23). Finally, God brought about a certain circumstance in the life of the Pharaoh so that he needed the very kind of help that Joseph had given to the man who had been in prison with him. This jogged the man's memory and he informed Pharaoh that he knew a man who could provide the very help that he wanted and needed. Hence, after many years of horrendous misrepresentation, mistreatment and abuse, Joseph was brought to Pharaoh and was able to provide the assistance he wanted. Pharaoh was so pleased that he gave the order to release Joseph from prison and exalt him to the position of prime minister of Egypt.

I mention this story because there is no indication that Joseph ever descended into utter despair, no evidence that he became bitter and angry, no evidence that he sought to get even or that he returned evil for evil to his brothers, to Potiphar or Potiphar's wife; or even to the official of Pharaoh who for a period of time forgot about him. During this rather lengthy period of time when he experienced a variety of stressors, Joseph must have been tempted to respond in many of the ungodly ways described in chapter five, but he didn't. To the contrary, when Joseph had the opportunity to get even with his brothers, he blessed them instead of cursing them, and comforted them rather than condemning them. When as prime minister he could have made it tough on Potiphar and his wife, there is no evidence that he did any such thing.

What kept Joseph from responding in ungodly ways to the stressors he experienced? To answer this question, we don't have to speculate or make guesses; Scripture tells us why: When he could have had his brothers executed, Joseph instead said, "Do not be grieved or angry with yourselves, because you sold me here, for God sent me before you to preserve life...God sent me before you to preserve for you a remnant in the earth, and to keep you alive by a great deliverance. Now, therefore, it was not you who sent me here, but God; and He has made me a father to Pharaoh and lord of all his household and ruler over all the land of Egypt" (Genesis 45:5-9). Later, in another attempt to comfort his brothers who had previously mistreated him, he said, "Do not be afraid ...you meant it for evil, but God meant it for good ... So therefore do not be afraid..."(Genesis 50:19-21).

Joseph knew that God was Sovereign and in charge of all things in general, and of his life in particular. He knew long before Paul ever penned those words that "God causes all things to work together for good to those who love God, to those who are called according to His purpose" (Romans 8:28). *He saw everything within the framework of God's sovereignty and that conviction was a key factor in his overcoming stress rather than being overcome by it.*

It was this same perspective that helped Paul to respond in a godly manner to the various and continuous stressors he faced. Some of the stress Paul faced came from enemies who frequently imprisoned and beat him for no valid reason at all. They whipped and scourged Paul so many times that he couldn't remember how many times he had been beaten. He was in constant danger of being killed. Frequently, he had little or no food to eat or safe water to drink. His enemies were so many and so determined to destroy him, that on an almost daily basis Paul didn't know if he was going to live or die (2 Corinthians 11:23-27). In addition to the stress that came from his enemies, he also faced pressures that came upon him from Christians. Often those who should have comforted and supported Him while he was suffering at the hands of the enemies of Christ, abandoned him, ignored him and were even ashamed to be identified with him. Some even tried to intensify his suffering and abuse by unjust criticism, by maligning his reputation, by misrepresenting his words; as well as by masking his actions and his motives. Perhaps no one except our Lord Jesus Christ ever experienced the intense and unrelenting pressure that Paul did (Philippians 1:12-18; 2 Timothy 4:10,16). Yet, Paul didn't lose heart, he was not overcome by the stressors he faced (2 Corinthians 4:8-16).

Why? Was it because he was some kind of superhuman being who had no feelings and didn't care what people thought of him? No, he responded as he did because he chose to see everything that happened to him within the framework of the sovereignty of a wise, loving, gracious, all-powerful God. It was because he knew and really believed that God was working all things according to the counsel of His own will and that God's will was ultimately good, perfect and acceptable (Romans 12:2). No matter what happened, Paul was convinced that God was good and that His God never makes a mistake. In 2 Corinthians 4:8 Paul acknowledged that there were times when he didn't fully understand what God was up to (2 Corinthians 4:8), but nonetheless, he was certain that whatever God was up to would ultimately work out for his good and God's glory. That knowledge helped him to overcome stress rather than being overcome by it.

What was it that sustained and supported William Carey during the many pressures and trials he experienced before he went to India and while he was there as a missionary? What was it that empowered John Bunyan to respond in a godly manner to being placed in prison for twelve and a half years for no other reason than that he wanted to preach the Gospel? What was it that enabled Jonathan Edwards to be kind and loving and compassionate toward the people of Northampton, Massachusetts when they maligned him and finally rejected him as their pastor? What is it that has helped Joni Erickson Tada to consistently over the years bear a sweet and radiant testimony for Christ while being paralyzed and restricted in her movements? What was it that has helped and is helping thousands of others to overcome the stressors that are part of the warp and woof of daily living in this present evil world? The answer: They choose to see everything within the framework of God's sovereignty.

Again and again in the years I have lived since I became a Christian in 1957, I have observed the practical value of this doctrine played out in the lives of people encountering various kinds of stress. For example, I think of how it helped a friend of mine as he went though a very trying time in his life. This man and his wife had gone into business with a brother who soon made some very unwise decisions. Because of his poor judgment, these people, through no fault of their own, ended up owing over $40,000 that was to be paid immediately. To top it off, the brother, who was responsible for the mess, decided to pull out of the business. So this friend and his wife were left with the responsibility to pay the debt. One problem: they had no money to pay the debt. Their creditors, of course, found out that they had just bought a house and threatened them with foreclosure if they didn't pay up immediately. As you can imagine, it was an extremely stressful situation.

Well, how did this couple handle the stress this situation provided?

That's the question I asked my friend, and he told me that while all this was happening, he and his wife experienced a number of temptations. They were tempted to worry and be depressed. They were tempted to become fearful. They were also tempted to become bitter and resentful at the brother who had gotten them into this mess, and even at God who had not prevented it from happening. But they were able to overcome the temptation and respond rather in faith.

I asked him, "What was of most help in keeping you from any of the unbiblical responses you just mentioned?" His answer was, "The main factor that preserved us from any of these responses was the confidence that God was in control and that he would fulfill the promise of Romans 8:28." He then went on to say that it took almost a year and a half before they began to actually understand anything about what God was up to in these happenings. Now at least they see in part, then they didn't have a clue about God's specific purposes. What they had was the truth of God's sovereignty and that was enough.

This biblical perspective on God's sovereignty over the whole of life has been a key factor in helping the people I've mentioned to respond to the stressors of life in a godly way, and what it did for them, it can and will do for you and me also. To overcome stress before it overcomes us, we must choose to see everything within the framework of God's sovereignty. We must train ourselves to think this way until that way of thinking becomes a habit pattern for us.

OVERCOMING FACTOR # 2

To win this battle over the stressors of life, we must also deliberately choose to give God thanks in the midst of everything and for everything.

I Thessalonians 5:18 says, "In everything give thanks." Ephesians 5:20 teaches us to give thanks always for all things in the name of our Lord Jesus Christ, to God, even the Father. Philippians 4:6 joins with these verses in stating that in everything we are to give thanks.

Following the counsel of these verses is the right thing to do for a number of reasons. For one thing, it's the right thing to do because God says we should do it and as His creatures and His children we should do what He commands. Then too, it's the right thing to do because God is worthy of continuous thanksgiving. The fact that giving thanks is the right thing to do ought to be enough motivation for us to get busy doing it.

But beyond the fact that it's the right thing to do, we ought to be constantly giving thanks because it's beneficial in several ways, one of them being overcoming the destructive consequences of stress.

The Psalmist in a number of places beautifully illustrates this practice of constantly giving thanks and the benefits thereof. One of these places is found in Psalm 34. In this Psalm, the psalmist begins by saying, "I will bless the Lord at all times; his praise shall continually be in my mouth." Putting this in vernacular terms it means: "I'm going to bless the Lord when the sun is shining, when it's raining, when I'm feeling good and when I'm feeling badly, when I'm being complimented and when I'm being criticized, when things are going well and when things are going poorly. In the context of the Psalm, the "all times" included times when he was experiencing fear and trouble, times when his enemies were out to get him. "All times" simply means: all times.

In particular, David wrote the Psalm when King Saul was pursuing him. In the midst of all that, David says, "I have made a commitment and I will keep that commitment whether I feel like it or not." At this point, David may not have known why God was allowing Saul to pursue him. Perhaps he didn't understand how this could be for his good. But the context of the Psalm indicates that even though there were some things he didn't fully understand, there were other things he did know. And for these he always had reason to bless the Lord.

What did the Psalmist know that would give him plenty of reason for praising God even in the midst of many stressors? He knew that, in spite of his circumstances, God was worthy of praise. He knew that even though he couldn't see him, God had sent his angel to encircle, protect and rescue him. He knew that God was good and that God would be a refuge for him. He knew that God would sustain and strengthen him. He knew that the eyes of the Lord were always upon him and that God's ears were always open to his cry. He knew that ultimately God would deal with his enemies. He knew that the Lord would ultimately deliver him out of his troubles. He knew that the Lord is near to the brokenhearted and that He saves those who are crushed in spirit. He knew that God would eventually deliver him from his afflictions. He knew that God would take care of his soul; and he knew that God would never condemn him (cf., Psalm 34:4– 22).

In the midst of his stressors, the Psalmist reflected on all the things he had to be thankful for; and blessed, praised, magnified, and exalted the Lord (Psalm 34:1-3). For him, giving thanks was the right thing to do. As evidenced in this Psalm, though he was experiencing many difficulties, he had many things for which he could and should be thankful. But, beyond the fact that giving thanks was the right thing for him to do, can you imagine the numerous personal benefits that this activity must have brought to him? What do you think happened in him as he reflected on the many reasons he had for giving thanks, or as he wrote down the things he had to be thankful for, and used his voice to audibly praise God in his private times, and in the presence of others (cf. Psalm 34:1-3)?

Without a doubt, the practice of continuously thinking about the reasons he had for giving thanks and then actually doing it helped him to avoid the common ungodly responses to stress and the consequences thereof.

One of my favorite Old Testament passages is found in 2 Chronicles 20. In this passage, Jehoshaphat, King of Judah and the citizens of Judah are facing a very stressful situation. Great coalitions of powerful neighboring nations have joined together to destroy Judah. At this point, they've prepared their armies and have arrived at the border of Judah. Israel, the northern and larger kingdom has already fallen. In comparison to them, Judah is a small and insignificant nation. From a human point of view they have little chance of resisting this coalition of nations.

Verse three describes Jehoshaphat's initial response. He was afraid. His initial reaction was terror, but that was not his continuing response. He, as it were, took himself by the scruff of the neck and said to himself: "Jehoshaphat, you can't continue to react in this way. You're reacting like a person who doesn't have Jehovah as his God." The text supports that idea in that it says that he "turned his attention to seek the Lord." His change in attitude didn't happen automatically. He had to make himself turn away from an exclusive focus on the problem, away from a preoccupation with the stressful situation to a focus on His God.

Verse four tells us that he gathered a group of praying people together to join with him in seeking the Lord in prayer. In the prayer, Jehoshaphat reflected on who God is, what He has (power, sovereignty, faithfulness, power, etc.) and what He has done for His people. Then in verse eighteen, after this prayer, we're told that he came together with an assembly of godly people and fell down and worshipped the Lord. Having spent some time in worship (reflecting on the worthiness of God), verse nineteen says they "stood up to praise the Lord with a very loud voice."

Verse twenty continues with a description of what Jehoshaphat did next. It tells us that he (and others) arose early the next day and gathered together for a message delivered by none other than Jehoshaphat himself. In the message, he exhorted his brethren to put their trust in the Lord and in His Word that was brought to them through God's prophets. In other words, he was exhorting them and himself to not just think about their danger, but even more importantly, to reflect on the trustworthiness of God and His Word. The message he delivered indicates that Jehoshaphat was seeking to personally see everything within the framework of God's sovereignty and was encouraging others to do the same.

Verses twenty-one and twenty-two add another significant detail about what Jehoshaphat did and encouraged others to do as they faced this very stressful situation. What did he do? He encouraged the people to sing, praise and give thanks to the Lord. He encouraged them to think about the lovingkindness and everlasting nature of God and His attributes.

How did Jehoshaphat respond to the stressful situation he faced? He put into practice the first two "overcoming stress factors" I'm explaining in this chapter. First, he chose to see everything within the framework of the sovereignty of God. Second, he chose to reflect on what he had to be thankful for, and then to actually in a verbal and even public way, give thanks to God.

I Corinthians 10:11 and Romans 15:4 inform us that what was written in an earlier time was written for our instruction. This account about Jehoshaphat is part of the earlier writings that Paul is referring to in these passages. In keeping with Paul's divinely inspired statements, we can conclude that we should react to stress the way he did. Through his example, we can be reproved for the wrong ways we respond to stress. Also, we can learn how to correct our wrong responses; and by reflecting on his example we can be trained so that responding rightly will become a pattern with us (2 Timothy 3:16).

Giving thanks always and in everything is a matter of obedience in that God commands us to do this very thing. Failing to do this is therefore an act of disobedience to the one called Lord. (I Thessalonians 5:18; Ephesians 5:20; Philippians 4:6; Colossians 4:2). Scripture, however, makes it clear that giving thanks is not only the right thing to do; it gives us many good and valid reasons for doing this. Psalm 147:2 tells us that we should give thanks because it's becoming. This means, of course, that praise is attractive, fitting and appropriate for believers (Psalm 147:2). Revelation 4:11 and Psalm 145:3 teach us that we should give thanks always because God is worthy that He should be praised at all times and in every situation (Revelation. 4:11; Psalm 145:3; Psalm 136; Revelation 5:9-13).

Psalm 147:2 contains an additional brief, yet very interesting and significant reason, for giving thanks always. This verse instructs us to praise the Lord because it's good and because it's pleasant or gracious. Certainly, it's morally good to praise the Lord in that He has commanded us to do it. But could the Psalmist be encouraging us to praise the Lord because it's good in another sense? Could he be encouraging us to praise the Lord because it's good and pleasant or beneficial for us?

Throughout Scripture, God often motivates us to obedience by telling us that obedience is good for us (James 1:22-25; Luke 11:28; Ephesians 6:1-3; Psalm 112:1; 128:1). Applying this fact to the matter of giving thanks, we can be sure that doing so is not only the right thing to do, it's also the good and pleasant thing to do. Without a doubt, people who make it a practice to do what the Psalmist did in Psalm 34, and what Jehoshaphat did in 2 Kings 20, will reap the benefit of overcoming the destructive consequences of stress.

In closing this chapter, I ask you, do you want to be a person who is an overcomer rather than a person who is overcome by stress? Mark it down, there's a way of escape from stress and the wrong responses and destructive consequences that follow them. The Psalmist found that way of escape and so did Jehoshaphat. You can and will find it also if you will actually put the biblical procedure described in this book into practice in your life.

APPLICATION QUESTIONS

>> In this chapter's presentation, important biblical factors for overcoming stress before it overcomes you were laid out. What were the two factors discussed in this chapter?

>> Explain the meaning of these factors.

>> Explain why practicing these two factors would help you or anyone else to overcome wrong responses to stress.

>> When being tempted to be stressed out, identify which of these factors you regularly practice.

>> Give examples of times and situations when you practiced these two factors.

» Explain the practical effect that practicing these two factors had on your life at that time.

» Identify which of these factors you are most prone to neglect when being tempted be stressed out.

» What will you do to make the biblical truths found in this chapter for overcoming stress before it overcomes you more of a reality in your life?

» Identify someone you know who is experiencing a lot of stress and is succumbing to the temptation to respond in unbiblical ways?

» Identify the ungodly ways they're responding and the destructive consequences they're experiencing. Identify the factors for overcoming presented in this session that they're not practicing.

» Plan how you could use this material to help these people to change their way of responding.

THE WAY OF ESCAPE – PART 2

Over the years in which I've been involved in counseling, I've had hundreds of people come to me experiencing the problem we are discussing in the last few chapters of this book. They come for help because, according to them, they're "stressed out," or "coming apart at the seams," or unable to sleep at night, or nervous, or anxious, or overwhelmed.

Because I'm a biblical counselor, most (not all) of the people I see in counseling are professing Christians. Yet, rather than overcoming the stressors in life, the stressors are overcoming them. They simply have not learned a biblical way of handling the pressures of life. Frankly, that is one of the reasons I decided to write this book. I want to help Christians to learn a biblical procedure for overcoming stress before it overcomes them.

In the last chapter, we began to discuss the details of this biblical procedure. We noted two of what we called overcoming factors. One of them was: That to overcome stress before it overcomes you, you must develop a pattern of seeing everything within the framework of God's sovereignty. The second factor was: That you must choose to develop a pattern of constantly giving thanks to God in everything and at all times.

In this chapter we move on to discuss several other key factors in the process of overcoming stress.

OVERCOMING FACTOR #3

To win this battle over the stressors of life, we should seek to discover God's purpose for the stressful situation. In the previous chapter, we noted that God uses the stressors of life to accomplish something good. (Romans 8:28,29; Jeremiah 29:11; James 1:2-5). This must be our attitude if we are thinking and functioning biblically; it must be our perspective of choice.

Sometimes, however, knowing exactly what God is up to through the stressor is not immediately clear to us. It doesn't happen as it does when you buy some kind of new appliance or piece of equipment. For example, when my wife and I recently bought a new automobile, we discovered that we didn't have a clue about the purpose of some of the gadgets, buttons and switches it had; and while we had a little understanding of what some of the other gadgets, buttons and switches were intended to do, we didn't know how to make the best use of them. Fortunately, there was an owner's manual to which we turned for help. Soon after buying the car, we made it a point to peruse the manual and now we can drive the car safely and use the gadgets in a beneficial way.

That's not the way it's with the stressors of life. They don't come with a little book that quickly and easily explains why God has allowed them to come into our lives or exactly how to benefit from them. There's no little book with a couple of pages that read, "You are going through this stressful situation because ...." That doesn't mean that they're not intended to serve a good purpose in our lives. Nor does it mean that we can't identify the purposes that God wants them to serve in our lives. It just means that we may have to do some biblical research (2 Timothy 2:15; Psalm 1:2; Isaiah 8:19-20). It means that we'll need to do some serious praying (James 1:5) and thinking to discover what the purposes are.

Many passages of Scripture present a variety of perspectives on God's purposes for trials in the lives of believers. Additionally, many sizeable volumes have been written to explain what the Scripture says about God's purposes for bringing various and numerous trials into our lives. In this book, it's not my purpose to be exhaustive in my explanation of God's purposes for the stressors that may come from our environment and circumstances, our own limitations and inadequacies, and from our relationships with people. Rather, my purpose is to give you a few of the broad purposes God often has in mind when we encounter various kinds of difficulties. My hope is that God will use what I write to stimulate you to consider whether God wants to use any of the stressors you experience to accomplish any of the purposes I suggest.

THE BOOMERANG, SOWING AND REAPING PRINCIPLE

When encountering the challenges of life that come from our relationships with people, we ought to think in terms of the sowing and reaping principle described in numerous passages of Scripture. "Whatever a man sows, this he will also reap (Galatians 6:7). "Do not condemn, and you will not be condemned; pardon, and you will be pardoned. Give, and it will be given to you…For by your standard of measure, it will be measured to you in return." (Luke 6:37-38) "And who is there to harm you if you prove zealous for what is good?"

Each of these verses suggest a very important general principle for dealing with interpersonal difficulties, namely, that the way people relate to us may be a mirror of what they see in our lives. When others are "standoffish" with us, it may be that they see us as being standoffish. If they're argumentative, critical or uncooperative with us, it may be that they perceive the same behaviors in us. This is not always the case, but it sometimes may be the case that we, by our own attitudes and actions, may be creating our own interpersonal environment.

When encountering stress from other people, we ought to at least consider the possibility of this boomerang or sowing and reaping effect. In keeping with this interpersonal relationship principle, our Lord Jesus Christ counsels us that when we are having problems in our relationships with people, we should "…notice the log in your own eye… first take the log out of your own eye, and then you will see clearly to take the speck out of your brother's eye" (Matthew 7:3-5).

In similar fashion, the book of Proverbs references the same phenomenon in a number of places. Note how this sampling of verses highlights this principle in an unmistakable way:

"A hot tempered man stirs up strife…"

"A soft answer turns away wrath, but harsh words stir up anger."

"Through presumption (i.e. pride) comes nothing but strife..."

"When pride comes, then comes dishonor..."

"Drive out the scoffer and contention will go out, even strife and dishonor will cease. He who loves purity of heart and whose speech is gracious the king is his friend." (Proverbs 15:15; 13:10; 11:2; 22:10-1)

These verses tell us that when the stress we face comes from our relationships with people, we should at least entertain the possibility that God is trying to get us to examine ourselves to see what we may be doing that either encourages or exacerbates our interpersonal problems. In other words, when someone is angry with us, God may be allowing this to occur so that we will learn to speak softly rather than harshly to people. When someone is demeaning, nasty and feisty with us, we should consider that perhaps God is allowing this to happen so that we will deal with our own internal and outwardly manifested pride. Since we know that God is working all things (including this interpersonal problem) together for good, when interpersonal stress occurs, our thinking should be, "Perhaps God wants to use what I'm experiencing as a mirror to make me aware of attitudes and behaviors I need to change, and thereby help me to become more conformed to the image of Jesus Christ, my Lord and Savior."

THE JAMES 1:2-5 ATTITUDE

Adopting a James 1:2-5 attitude toward the stressors of life is an essential part of overcoming stress before it overcomes us. In this passage, James clearly states that for us to overcome the destructive influence of stress, it's important for us to know that God will use various kinds of trials to do several very beneficial things in our lives. First, James wants us to know that God will use these trials to test us. That is, trials will help to assess the reality and strength of our faith, commitment, devotion, and of our submission to Him. Certainly, the testing referred to here is all for our benefit not God's, because God, being omniscient, already knows the facts about us.

Second, James tells us that God will use the stressors of life to produce the very important quality of perseverance or steadfastness. Instability and inconstancy, constant vacillation and deterioration seem to be the order of the day for many. Like the Galatians (cf. Galatians 3:3-5), there are many who seem to begin well, but have no staying power. They lack persevering power.

Our Lord Jesus Christ described these people in Matthew 13 as people who have no firm root in themselves, but are only "temporary believers" for when affliction or persecution arises they quickly fall away. For these people, their faith was put to the test by the trials they experienced. Their response to that testing proved that their faith was spurious and, in fact, non-existent. Interestingly, according to James, for other people the same trials can serve a radically different purpose. For others, the trials can serve the extremely useful purpose of producing a quality that cannot be developed apart from the experience of stress. For these people, the trials generate perseverance and steadfastness, qualities that are absolutely essential if we are to experience the blessings of God and run the race of the Christian life successfully (Hebrews 10:36; 12:1)

In addition to these two overcoming stress perspectives that James has mentioned, he goes on to tell us that to overcome the destructive effects of wrong responses to stress we must recognize that God wants to use these stressors to make us "perfect and complete, lacking in nothing." (NASB) In commenting on this phrase, Simon Kristemaker writes:

What does "perfect" mean? Certainly it does not mean "without sin." James 3:2 says, "We all stumble in many ways. If anyone is never at fault in what he says, he is a perfect man, able to keep his whole body in check." James intends to convey the concept of wholeness, that is, "not lagging behind in any point." Addressing the Philippians, Paul also uses the expression *perfect*. The New International Version translates it "mature" (Philippians 3:15). "All of us who are mature should take such a view of things." With respect to the readers of Paul and James' letters, the term *perfect* means "mature."

A synonym of "mature" is the word *complete*. In the name of Jesus, Peter healed the lame man who daily sat begging at Solomon's colonnade. Luke writes that this beggar was given complete healing (Acts 3:16). The crippled man's feet and ankles became strong so that he functioned as a complete human being without handicap.

The phrase *not lacking anything* is synonymous with the preceding *complete*, which expresses the concept that all parts are functioning. Although both terms state the same concept, the first does so positively; the second, negatively. [1]

Implicit in the directions that James gives for overcoming stress before it overcomes us, is the idea that success in this endeavor requires that we understand our own deficiencies; that we realize we are lacking in many things. It requires that we understand that the trials we face are God's way of uncovering the existence and nature of our deficiencies, so that those deficiencies may be corrected. It suggests that the trials we encounter can help us to identify our pockets of immaturity and our areas of incompleteness; the areas in our lives where we are most lacking in being like Jesus Christ. Getting the most benefit out of our trials requires us to recognize that the stressors don't make us immature or incomplete; they simply reveal where this is already true so that we can seek God's help in correcting these deficiencies in our lives.

In my own life, as I have encountered some of the various stressors James is referring to, I have found it very helpful to focus on a verbal picture of what God wants every Christian to be. Ultimately we know that God wants to make us like Jesus Christ (Romans 8:29; Ephesians 4:13-15). Maturity and completeness means that we are like Jesus. Immaturity and incompleteness means being unlike Jesus in any area of our lives. But while all of this is true, the concept of being like Christ may seem rather vague and hard to get our arms around. "What would Jesus do?" is a wonderful concept, but without specifics to fill in the blanks, it may be somewhat useless. Asking the question, "How am I unlike Jesus," is a good practice for identifying what God may want to do in my life through stressors. Unfortunately, it doesn't go far enough, and really isn't very helpful unless I know specifics about what Jesus is like.

To make this concept of being like Jesus really meaningful, I have personally found it very useful to compare myself to the verbal picture of a Christian given in several passages of Scripture. Doing this has been useful to me because each of these passages gives us a wonderful verbal picture of what Jesus is like. Many passages of Scripture could be used for this purpose, but I will mention only two of them. One of these passages is Matthew 5:3-12 where a Christian is described as a person who is *poor in spirit, grieved over sin, gentle or meek, hungering and thirsting after righteousness, merciful, pure in heart, a peacemaker, and so committed to righteousness that he will suffer rather than be unrighteous.* My response to the stressors I face will either reveal the *presence or absence* of these qualities in my life. My response will bring to the surface the areas in which I'm immature and incomplete (i.e., unlike Jesus). Then, having identified the way in which I'm not like Jesus, I can confess my sin, seek God's help and commit myself to disciplining myself for the purpose of godliness (I Timothy 4:7) which, of course, means becoming like Jesus.

Another passage that I use in the same way is Galatians 5:22-23, about the fruit of the Spirit. Scripture says that Jesus is the perfect example of someone who is filled with the Spirit (Isaiah 11:2-5; John 3:34; Acts 10:38). Therefore, as might be expected, His life was a perfect example of one that was filled to overflowing with the fruit of the Spirit. The Lord Jesus Christ was the ultimate personification of love, joy, peace, patience, kindness, goodness, faithfulness, gentleness and self-control.

As I encounter various stressors in life, I try to focus on the truths found in James 1:2-4, that God wants to use the stressors in my life to reveal my deficiencies, and also make me more like Jesus. I try to deliberately meditate on the fact that my response will bring to the surface the areas in which I'm immature and incomplete (i.e., unlike Jesus), and that when I use Galatians 5:22-23 as the evaluative grid for determining ways in which I'm unlike Jesus, the stressors can be turned into an asset in my Christian life.

Using Galatians 5:22-23 as an evaluative grid, I ask myself: "Is my potential or actual response revealing a lack of love, joy, peace, patience, kindness, goodness, gentleness, faithfulness or self control?" Then, having finished identifying the particular areas in which I'm unlike Christ, I go on to confess my sin, seek God's help, commit myself to disciplining myself for the purpose of godliness, and develop a plan for making that godliness more of a reality in my life (I Timothy 4:7).

I wish I could say that I have always handled the stressors in my life in this way, but honesty compels me to admit that I haven't. I can honestly say, however, that whenever I have responded in this way (and I'm growing), I have benefited, rather than been destroyed by them. Moreover, I can confidently say because it's based on solid rock biblical truth, that if you will approach the stressors in your life in this way, you will make real progress in overcoming stress before it overcomes you.

OVERCOMING FACTOR # 4

To overcome stress before it overcomes you, you must seek to discover what God wants you to do in the midst of the stressful situation. According to the Bible, real biblical change in any area of life is always a two-factored process; it's a matter of putting some things off and putting some things on. For example, Ephesians 4:31 which instructs us to put off "all bitterness and wrath and anger and clamor and slander"... along "with all malice" (all unbiblical responses to the stressors we face) is followed by Ephesians 4:32 which tells us to put on tenderheartedness, kindness and forgiveness. That is, eliminating the wrong responses is not enough. These wrong responses must be replaced with the right responses; it's *displacement* by *replacement* and *dehabituation* by *rehabituation*. We are to stop responding the wrong way by learning to respond the right way.

Philippians 4:6-9 tells us that the wrong response of anxiety is to be replaced with the right kind of prayer, thinking and actions. Colossians 3:8-14 informs us that we should get rid of the wrong responses of anger, wrath, malice, slander, abusive and deceitful speech and put on in its place a heart of compassion, kindness, humility, gentleness, patience, forbearance, forgiveness and love. In all these passages and many more, the Bible challenges us to not only focus on what we shouldn't do, but, even more importantly, on what we *should* do.

What this means is that when we encounter stressors, we should exercise emotional, cognitive and behavioral self-control and make ourselves deliberately think about what an appropriate godly, biblical response would be. Instead of allowing ourselves to have a knee-jerk reaction, we should develop the habit of bringing every thought into captivity and making it obedient to Christ (2 Corinthians 10:5). When under stress, we should discipline ourselves to ask the question, "What would God have me do; how should I respond?"

As we do this, several things will happen:

· We will be obeying and renewing our minds with Scripture.
· We and our responses to the stressors will be transformed.
· We will discover, prove and approve the good, perfect and acceptable will of God (Romans 12:2).

At this point, I want to illustrate what it looks like in practice to utilize the overcoming factors I've mentioned thus far by telling you about how they were implemented by a young lady we'll call "Sally." When Sally came to me for counseling, she told me of her past involvement in a satanic cult, lesbianism, and a lot of other destructive and ungodly experiences. She also informed me that she recently had become a Christian, who now wanted to put off her old ungodly patterns of life and put on godly attitudes and behaviors. One of the problems she faced in doing this was related to a woman with whom she had a lesbian affair.

Sally had clearly told this woman (we'll call her "Susan") that she had become a Christian and wanted nothing to do with her former manner of life. Unfortunately, this former partner in sin would not let her alone. Susan just kept coming back to harass her. She would go to where this young lady worked and follow her home. When they arrived at her apartment, Susan would jump out of the car and try to persuade Sally to return to their immoral relationship.

On one occasion, when Sally had stopped at a stop light behind several other cars, Susan ran up to her car, forced open the door and threatened her with bodily harm unless she returned to her. I told her to report this woman to the police and ask for police protection. I also informed her that she should enlist the elders and people of her church in doing whatever they could to provide safety for her. I suggested that she should try to get other people to go with her to as many activities as she possibly could.

In spite of all this, Susan continued to stalk her, looking for opportunities when she could harass her, and hopefully pressure her into returning. One day when she came for her counseling appointment, she told me that Susan had again accosted her when she was coming out of a restaurant. She said that Susan had abused her physically and threatened her verbally. I asked her, "How did you respond? How were you affected?" She indicated that she had become very alarmed and afraid, not knowing to what lengths Susan might go in carrying out her threats.

While Sally was relating her experience to me, I identified with her difficult situation and reflected on how I would be tempted to think and feel if I were experiencing what she was experiencing. As I listened to her, I thought of a passage in I Peter that seemed to be a match for what Sally was going through, a passage that could provide the help and direction she needed. When she finished her description of what was happening in her life, I reminded her that God has given us in His Word everything we need for life and godliness (2 Peter 1:3-4). I told her that as I listened to her, I couldn't help but think of a passage in I Peter that seemed to be very appropriate for her at this time in her life. I then asked her to turn with me to that passage, I Peter 3:13–16. I explained to her that this passage, indeed all of I Peter, was written to people who were suffering for the same reason she was suffering. They were suffering for righteousness; they were suffering because they had taken their stand for Christ (3:14; 4:16).

We studied I Peter 3:13 which suggests that when we are continuously doing good, we are much less likely to be mistreated or persecuted. We then went on to look at verse fourteen which indicates that there are times when, even though we are zealously doing what is good, God, for His own good purposes, may still allow us to suffer. We also noticed that this statement about the possibility that doers of good will suffer is followed by an assurance of blessing for those who suffer for righteousness sake. We talked about why and how the person who suffers for righteousness might be blessed, noting some of the reasons why this person is blessed, paying close attention to the blessings mentioned in the immediate (I Peter 3:15-16) and larger context of I Peter.

Having done this, we focused on God's instructions about what we should and should not do when we experience the hardships found in I Peter 3:14-16. We noted that verse 14 tells us what we shouldn't do (what we should put off). Specifically, we reflected on Peter's challenge not to allow their threats and abuses to intimidate us and cause us to be despondent.

We then spent some time discussing verses fifteen and sixteen, which provide the directions (the put ons) for overcoming the wrong, destructive responses of verse fourteen. According to Peter, we must put on right responses as well as put off wrong responses. In fact, his point is that we put off by putting on. The word "but" with which verse 15 begins calls our attention to the fact that what he is about to say is vitally connected to what he has just said. Namely, that instead of responding to stressors with fear and despair, we should sanctify Christ as Lord in our hearts. That is, we should choose to see everything that happens to us within the framework of our Lord's sovereignty.

We explored together the implication of this, specifically that recognizing and understanding that our Savior is Christ and Lord, and that this is the antidote to being overcome by the stressors of life. With Sally, I discussed the relevance of this to the experience of being mistreated and threatened. In context, I mentioned that it means when we are called on to go through hard times, we must meditate on the fact that Christ is Lord of everything and everybody.

This means that in every situation and at all times, we should reflect on the fact that Christ is ruling, that He is still in control, and that He has all authority in heaven and on earth. I then asked her how all of this might apply to her situation with Susan. She made the connection. I explained to her that this means that Christ has authority over Susan, and therefore, Christ can restrain her. It means that Susan is not Lord and you must not think of her in that way. Furthermore, I stated that if and when you think of Susan in this way, fear would control you. On the basis of this text, I told her that when she is tempted to allow fear to overcome her, she should deliberately at that moment reflect on the fact that Christ is Lord of all, and that He is Lord of you.

I admonished her to do several things: First, she must choose to see everything within the framework of the sovereignty of God. Second, she must deliberately choose to thank God for His power, for His promises, and for His watch care over her. I told her that as she does this, she must remember that God is up to something in allowing this to happen; and, according to His Word, what He is up to is something that will ultimately be good for her and will bring glory to Him (Romans 8:28; Romans 11:36). I urged her to think about what God may want to do in her and through her by means of the Susanic stressor (James 1:2-4).

Then having exposited and applied the truth of verse fifteen, we moved on to note another thing God says we must do if we would overcome the stressor of difficult circumstances in verse sixteen: Instead of focusing exclusively on the horror of the situation, we should focus on doing good and making sure we behave in a God pleasing way. In other words, the passage challenges us to bring our thoughts into subjection and make ourselves think about what God wants us to do and on how God would have us to act so that we might be a testimony for Him. In the context of our difficulties, we should be thinking about what it means to sanctify Christ as Lord. As we face stressful situations, we should devote our attention to planning and doing good instead of thinking mainly about the horrific nature of the problem. In times like these, we should be proactive, rather than reactive. We should be asking, "Lord, what would you have me to do? How can I show the glory of Christ in my responses to their wickedness?

That's what Sally needed to hear in the midst of her stressful situation. What was presented to her was, and still is, God's plan for handling the stressors of life. Should you be wondering what happened in reference to the Susan harassment issue, I'm glad to be able to say that as Sally continued in her Christian life, Susan began to realize that her threats and attempts at intimidation were useless. She backed off and the attempts at intimidation ceased.

Sally, I say, needed to hear these truths. So do you and I. Mark it down and accept it as fact; as long as you are in this world, you will encounter a variety of stressors. Furthermore, you may count on it that as you face these stressors, you will be tempted to respond in an unbiblical way. Moreover, you can also be assured that when you faithfully and believingly follow the biblical procedure I presented to Sally, you will be able to overcome stress before it overcomes you.

OVERCOMING FACTOR #5

Over the years I have met and counseled many people who were coming apart at the seams because they were unnecessarily putting themselves in a "stressor situation." Some were doing this by trying to do too many things. Some were doing this by failing to schedule and plan. Some were doing this by going places they should not have gone. Some were doing this by associating with the wrong kind of people. Some were doing this by thinking that every need was a command from God for them to fulfill. Some were doing this out of fear that if they didn't do something, it wouldn't get done, or certainly it wouldn't be done well. Some were doing this because they wanted people to think well of them or because they were afraid to say no. Some were doing this because being busy and overloaded made them feel important.

The reason people unnecessarily put themselves in potentially stressful situations may vary. If the people who feel pressured by the thought that they have too much to do want to prevent being overcome by stress, it's helpful for them to practice some self-examination to discover the main reason for their stress. These people should be asking themselves, "Am I being stressed out for any of the aforementioned reasons or for any other reasons that weren't even mentioned?" Then they should seek to discover God's perspective on their reason for putting themselves in an unnecessarily stressful situation, and follow that by making the changes that God would have them make.

One thing is certain: God will never call on us to do more than what we, by His grace, are able to do (Philippians 4:13; 2 Corinthians 3:5-6; 9:8; Colossians 1:29). The words Jesus spoke in defense of a certain woman who was criticized by others for something she had done are extremely encouraging for all of us as we seek to live in this present world. In defending her, Jesus told her critics to leave her alone because she has done what she could (Mark 14:8).

Those words of Jesus are extremely significant for us. They indicate that our Lord didn't expect her to do what she couldn't do; only what she was able to do. So it is with us. God expects us to do what we can, no more and no less. This we must learn if we are going to overcome stress.

For example, if we have interpersonal relationship pressures, our responsibility is, "So far as it depends on us, (to) be at peace with all men." We must "pursue the things which make for peace and the building up of one another" (Romans 12:18; 14:19). These things we must do; the things that are likely to facilitate peace with other people. Pursuing the things that make for peace means that a husband or wife who has serious conflicts with a spouse should consistently seek to implement the directives of I Peter 3:1-7. That's their responsibility. That they can do. However, what they cannot and should not do is try and make that spouse to be at peace with them. If they think that they must and can fix the problem, they're trying to do more than they can do and will end up being stressed out. They must fulfill their God directed responsibility and then rely on God to do what they can't do.

Similarly, if there are things that are not being done at work or at church, then people must learn to prioritize and schedule, they must learn to use their time wisely; they must work heartily in accordance with their priorities as unto the Lord and not try to do more than they could or should do (Colossians 3:23-25; Ephesians 6:5-9). This means they must learn to say yes to the things they can and should do and no to the things that are not their primary responsibilities. They must say no to the things they can't presently do because of a lack of time or skill. Perhaps, at another time, they will be able to do these things, but not so at the present time. Failure to plan their work according to priorities and failure to work their plan according to those priorities will certainly put them in an unnecessarily stressful situation

OVERCOMING FACTOR # 6

In my book, *A Homework Manual for Biblical Living, Volume 1*, I mention that many times we become annoyed, angry, and resentful because we think some right of ours is being denied. To overcome this propensity, I encourage people to:

Discern which rights of yours are being denied or neglected in this situation. Do you think you have a right to be respected, and is that why you are becoming upset because your wife won't fulfill your wishes? Do you think you have a right to be appreciated, and is that why you are becoming resentful toward someone who has criticized you or won't express his indebtedness to you? Identify what you are being denied and turn the matter over to God. You belong to Him. He knows what you really need (Philippians 4:19). Trust Him to take care of you. He knows what things you have need of even before you ask (Matthew 6:25-34). Believe that God is wiser than you. He knows much better than you what you really need, and He will supply what you need if you handle matters His way.

Turning your rights over to God doesn't mean you must become a doormat. It does not mean that you never make your desires known, or that you never oppose, rebuke, insist, exhort, or seek to correct a person. It does mean that you seek to do what you do in a biblical, God-honoring fashion; for biblical, God-honoring reasons; out of biblical, God-honoring motives. It does mean that after you have done all that you may legitimately do, you leave the results with God and believe that He will bring to pass what is right and good for you. God's promise is that they who fear Him and seek Him will not lack any good thing (Psalm 34:8-10). You must fulfill your biblical responsibilities and then leave your rights to God. When He gives them back to you, consider them to be privileges and thank Him for them.[1]

I once read the story of a man who was known as a great worrier. When you met him, worry was written all over his face. Wherever he went, people would hear him complaining and groaning about this or that or the other thing. It seemed that nothing ever suited him. But then one day when someone who hadn't seen him for a while met him, he noticed that there was something different about this man. He was struck by the fact that this man wasn't groaning, grumbling and complaining. What he saw was a pleasant expression and a smile on his face. Immediately, he recognized that this man was really quite different from the person he had known. So, he asked him, "What's happened to you?" The man responded that he had hired someone else to do his worrying for him.

"How much does he charge for that service?"

"About $200.00 a day," was his reply.

"Wow, that's great, but how can you afford to pay this person $200.00 a day. Why, that's $1400 a week!"

"Oh", said the man, "I can't afford to pay him that amount, but I don't worry about it at all because that's not my problem. That's what I pay him to do. It is his responsibility to do the worrying for me."

Well, my friends, that's a fictitious story, but it has a real point for us as Christians: We've turned all our rights over to Him. As I Cor. 6:20 tells us, we're not our own. We've been bought with a price. We belong to Him and He has said, "Don't worry. You have a Heavenly Father who knows all about your situation; who cares and has said that if you take care of fulfilling your God-given responsibilities, He'll take care of your needs and rights. (I Peter 5:7; Philippians 4:19; Matthew 6:18-34; Hebrews 13:5-6; Psalm 34:8-10).

At the beginning of this section on overcoming stress, I asserted that everyone who lives in this world will encounter stressors. They simply can't be avoided. Therefore, if you are to overcome these stressors so that they do not wreak havoc in your life and relationships, you must have a well-grounded biblical procedure, which you will faithfully use whenever you face these stressors. In this book, I have presented what I'm convinced is a godly way of responding to stressors of life.

I'm convinced that this biblically-based procedure will work when you use it. It will work because it's based on biblical truth. The question is not, "Will it work?" The question is, "Will you use it?" God grant that you and I will respond with a resounding, "Yes!" If we do, we will become people, who in accordance with I Peter 3:15 and 16, cause others to wonder what makes us so different; it will cause people who reject our Christ and our Christian lifestyle to be put to shame. To God be the glory, great things He has done and great things He will do, as we love, trust, and obey Him.

APPLICATION/DISCUSSION QUESTIONS

» In this session's presentation, some additional important biblical factors for overcoming stress before it overcomes you were laid out.

» What were the factors discussed in this chapter?
Summarize the meaning of these factors.

» Explain why practicing these factors would help you or anyone else to overcome wrong responses to stress.

» Identify which of these factors you regularly practice when tempted to be "stressed out."

» Give examples of times and situations when you practiced these factors.

» Explain the practical effect that practicing these factors had on your life at that time.

» Identify which of these factors you are most prone to neglect when being tempted be stressed out.

» Are there times when you overextend yourself and try to do too much? Are there things you are saying yes to that you shouldn't be saying yes to? Do you operate your life and use your time and energy in keeping with God's priorities for your life? What are God's priorities for your life? Are there things you should change? If so, what? And what must you do to make those changes?

» When you think of the verbal picture of a Christian described in the beatitudes (Matthew 5:1-12) which of them are you most concerned about developing more of in your life? How could stressors help you to achieve this?

» What perceived rights are being denied when you respond wrongly to stressors? What improvements can you make to improve in your response to denied rights?

» What will you do to make the biblical truths found in this chapter for overcoming stress before it overcomes you more of a reality in your life?

» Identify someone you know who is experiencing a lot of stress and is succumbing to the temptation to respond in unbiblical ways?

» Identify the ungodly ways they're responding and the destructive consequences they're experiencing. Identify the factors for overcoming presented in this session that they're not practicing.

» How could you use this material to help these people to change their way of responding?

1   Wayne Mack, *A Homework Manual for Biblical Living, Volume 1* (Phillipsburg, NJ: P&R Publishers, 1979), p. 8

Author's Bio

Dr. Mack is a graduate of Wheaton College, the Philadelphia Seminary, and Westminster Theological Seminary. He has been married to his wife, Carol, since 1957. They have four adult children and thirteen grandchildren.